A GENERAL APPROACH TO MACROECONOMIC POLICY

Also by J.O.N. Perkins

ANTI-CYCLICAL POLICY IN AUSTRALIA
AUSTRALIA IN THE WORLD ECONOMY
AUSTRALIAN MACROECONOMIC POLICY, 1974–85
THE AUSTRALIAN FINANCIAL SYSTEM AFTER THE CAMPBELL REPORT
BRITAIN AND AUSTRALIA: Economic Relationships in the 1950s
CONTEMPORARY MACROECONOMICS (*with R.S. Jones*)
CRISIS-POINT IN AUSTRALIAN ECONOMY POLICY
THE DEREGULATION OF THE AUSTRALIAN FINANCIAL SYSTEM
INTERNATIONAL POLICY FOR THE WORLD ECONOMY
*THE MACROECONOMIC MIX IN THE INDUSTRIALISED WORLD
*THE MACROECONOMIC MIX TO STOP STAGFLATION
MACROECONOMIC POLICY IN AUSTRALIA
*NATIONAL INCOME AND ECONOMIC PROGRESS
(*editor with Duncan Ironmonger and Tran Van Hoa*)
STERLING AND REGIONAL PAYMENTS SYSTEMS
*UNEMPLOYMENT, INFLATION AND NEW MACROECONOMIC POLICY

* *Also published by Macmillan*

A General Approach to Macroeconomic Policy

J.O.N. Perkins
Professor Emeritus
University of Melbourne, Australia

M
MACMILLAN

First edition 1990

Published by
MACMILLAN ACADEMIC AND PROFESSIONAL LTD
Houndmills, Basingstoke, Hampshire RG21 2XS
and London
Companies and representatives
throughout the world

Typeset by P&R Typesetters Ltd, Salisbury, Wilts, UK
Printed in Hong Kong

British Library Cataloguing in Publication Data
Perkins, J. O. N. (James Oliver Newton), 1924–
A general approach to macroeconomic policy.
1. Macroeconomic policies
I. Title
339

ISBN 0–333–48566–1

To all those econometricians who are asking, and trying to answer, the right questions about the relative effects of different instruments on the various macroeconomic objectives

Contents

List of Tables

Preface

This book complements earlier studies by the present author by extending the analysis of macroeconomic policy from the need to deal with two problems (inflation and unemployment) to include also either the state of the current account of the balance of payments, or a broader objective that includes the level of investment as well as the state of the balance of payments.

It draws upon the results of a number of macroeconometric models to throw light on the relative effects of a number of different macroeconomic policy instruments on each of these objectives; and suggests a framework that is broader than that usually adopted, in which to consider macroeconomic policy decisions to deal with these various objectives simultaneously.

The work was begun during a period spent in University College, London, whose hospitality is gratefully acknowledged. I benefited considerably from discussions with economists at the European Economic Community (EEC), the Organisation for Economic Cooperation and Development (OECD) and the University of Warwick; and also from the comments of participants in seminars and conferences at the University of Adelaide, the Australian National University, Helsinki University, the University of Oslo, the University of Stockholm and the University of Melbourne. My colleagues, especially Bob Jones and Ian McDonald, provided much helpful discussion and useful comments. The usual caveat of course applies.

Special thanks are owed to Duncan Ironmonger for suggestions and for assistance with proofreading.

Finally, I would acknolwedge the unfailingly cheerful and efficient secretarial services of the University of Melbourne mainframe computer.

J.O.N.P.
Melbourne

1 Introduction

The current macroeconomic problem of the world economy is to reduce unemployment and restore and maintain a healthy rate of economic growth without making inflation worse.

This need to raise growth without unduly increasing inflation is a far more urgent matter for primary-exporting countries, especially those with a high level of international indebtedness, than it is for the main industrialised countries, whose policies have the principal role in determining the world economic situation – many of which may be reasonably satisfied with the prevailing rate of economic growth. One reason why the more industrialised countries have much less incentive to look for policies that increase growth than do other countries is that a relatively low rate of economic growth in the industrialised countries to some extent actually helps to maintain the living standards of those people in them with jobs, by holding down the prices of primary commodities. On the other hand, the countries that suffer most from a low rate of world economic growth include not only most of the countries with relatively low living standards, but also primary-exporting countries with higher living standards, such as Australia and New Zealand.

But the external economic problems of high and rising indebtedness, from which many of those countries are suffering, present problems also for the more industrialised countries, especially for their financial systems. In the long run, all countries would benefit by having low unemployment and a high rate of growth.

However, policy makers in the richer and more industrialised countries fear that a high rate of growth and low unemployment could be restored only by measures that would increase the upward pressure on the price level.

But it seems likely that there are combinations of macroeconomic instruments that could increase the rate of economic growth without increasing the upward pressure on the price level (and even with some downward pressure on prices). The difficulty is that the approaches to the discussion of macroeconomic policy that have become widely accepted assume – implicitly or explicitly – that measures that stimulate growth by reducing unemployment are bound to make inflation worse. But this is not necessarily so. For there are a number of reasonable assumptions about the respective effects of the different macroeconomic policy instruments on inflation and unemployment, on the basis of which combinations of measures exist that can reduce unemployment and stimulate growth without exerting upward pressure on the price level over the period in which the change of policy is occurring and over subsequent years. In order to allow for such possibilities a much broader framework for discussing macroeconomic policy issues is required than has normally been applied in the past.

This book sets out the various combinations of assumptions on the basis of which a policy is available to reduce unemployment without worsening inflation; and it turns out that only on very special asumptions is no such mix of policy measures available.

Unfortunately, most macroeconomic policy discussion has been dominated by sets of assumptions about the effects of the various instruments of policy upon the objectives of employment (or growth) and on the price level that imply that no combinations of measures are available that will stimulate output without worsening inflation.

In particular, for about a decade policy discussion was dominated by the opposing views of 'monetarists' and 'Keynesians'. The former inclined to the view that fiscal measures – whether by changes in taxation or government outlays – could not influence either employment or the price level without an increase in monetary growth; whereas the Keynesians tended to believe that all the available measures – tax cuts, government outlays, and an easing of monetary policy – could affect employment; and that the extent to which those measures would affect the price level depended manly, or even solely, on how close the economy was to full employment (together with the rate at which full employment was being approached). Both these extreme views shared the characteristic that if either of them was valid there would not be combinations of measures available that could deal simultaneously with both inflation and unemployment; and it was therefore not surprising that policy makers came to act as if no such combinations of policy measures were available. But these approaches failed to take account of a number of reasonable combinations of assumptions – many of them in some sense or other intermediate between the Keynesian and monetarist positions – on the basis of which policies would be available to deal simultaneously with both inflation and unemployment.

More recently, most economists have come to see that neither the monetarist nor the Keynesian view is wholly convincing. On the one hand, the monetarist view that fiscal measures cannot affect employment would not now be widely held (if, indeed, it ever was); and, on the other hand, most observers would also agree that the extent of upward pressure on the price level in any given period is affected not only by how close the economy is to full employment, but also by the setting of particular instruments, including that of monetary policy. Some writers have taken account of the possibility that high tax rates may have certain cost-increasing effects not shared by reductions in government outlays: but generally speaking there is very little in the literature that gives proper recognition to the fact that fiscal policy requires to be divided into at least two sub-divisions – taxation and government outlays – as those two different fiscal instruments may each have very different relative effects from one another on particular macroeconomic objectives.

This means that most approaches to the analysis of macroeconomic policy are seriously defective as guides to policy makers. For the discussion of macroeconomic policy has consequently failed to take due account of the very different possibilities that open up for dealing simultaneously with both the principal macroeconomic policy problems (inflation and unemployment) once the combinations of assumptions at the monetarist and Keynesian extremes have been abandoned.

The approach of the present book is, therefore, to take account of the possibility – indeed, the probability – that each of the main macroeconomic instruments, monetary policy, taxation, and government outlays, may have different effects from one another on prices for a given effect on real output or employment. A sufficiently general approach to the discussion of macroeconomic policy needs to envisage the possibility that each of these broad instruments (and perhaps also subdivisions of them) may increase, reduce, or have a negligible effect upon one or both of the two main macroeconomic objectives; as well as of the probability that their relative effects on each objective may vary from one instrument to another. This is the first sense in which the approach in this book is more 'general' than that normally employed in discussions of macroeconomic policy.

In addition, if the combination of macroeconomic instruments that is chosen to deal with the two main macroeconomic objectives has undesirable effects on the allocation of resources between current consumption, on the one hand, and investment (which facilitates future growth), on the other, this also needs to be taken into account in reaching decisions about the combination of macroeconomic instruments that is most desirable in any given situation. Investment by a country includes the investment that it is undertaking in the rest of the world (its current account surplus) or less its net borrowing (the current account deficit) as well as the real investment undertaken within its borders. The level of investment (domestic and external) is therefore also introduced into the discussion in this book as a third objective, and a framework broad enough to include it is suggested.

There is a further sense in which the framework of thinking about macroeconomic policy needs to be more general than is customary. This is to take account of the fact that in particular countries and periods it might be thought desirable to raise output while not affecting prices, or to reduce the upward pressure on prices without affecting output – or to raise *or reduce* output, and to reduce *or increase* the upward pressure on prices. The framework suggested here is general enough to be applicable to these cases also, if the obvious changes are made to the arguments. But for simplicity, and to maximise the relevance of the analysis to current (and prospective future) problems, the exposition will concentrate for the most part upon situations where the aim is to raise output (or employment) and to exert downward pressure on prices (or, at any rate, to avoid increasing the upward pressure on prices). But when a third objective is introduced – which may be the state of the current account of the balance of payments, or the level of investment at any given level of output, or a combination of the two – the analysis will be applied both to cases of countries that wish to increase this third objective of policy and to cases of governments that wish to reduce it (for example, to move the current account of their balance of payments either towards surplus *or* towards deficit, and to raise *or* lower the level of real investment at any given level of total output or employment).

In addition to setting out the possible combinations of assumptions that might be made, and the implications for policy of those sets of assumptions, evidence from a number of sources is drawn upon to suggest which sets of assumptions are most likely to be realistic.

Finally, the principal implications of the discussion are suggested, both for individual countries' policies and for an international cooperative approach to macroeconomic policy.

2 Macroeconomic Policy with Two Objectives: Basic Arguments

The principal problem for macroeconomic policy makers since the late 1960s has been to maintain or increase the level of real output or employment without increasing the upward pressure on prices (and, if possible, reducing it). In subsequent discussion this second objective will be termed 'reducing inflation'. It is to be understood as meaning 'reducing the increase in prices, as measured by the change in the consumer price index or the gross national product/gross domestic product (GNP/GDP) price index (or "GDP deflator") over the period that is of interest to the policy maker'. The main obstacle to taking sufficiently expansionary action to reduce unemployment has been the fear that any form of macroeconomic stimulus would be bound to increase the upward pressure on prices, rather than a conviction that there are no more available resources with which to increase real output and employment.

If the *only* influence over changes in the general level of prices were the extent to which the economy was operating at, or near, full employment, or the speed with which it was approaching (or falling below) full employment, then these two objectives would amount to a single one. Even if the extent of upward pressure on prices depended only on the rate of change in the level of unemployment (or on both its level and its rate of change), these two objectives would, again, amount to one. But it is only if all possible combinations of macroeconomic instruments with which a given level (or change) in real output or employment is attained have the same effect on the rise in the price level over the relevant period that the two objectives are inseparable. The present chapter argues that this is unlikely to be a valid assumption on *a priori* grounds, while Chapter 3 outlines some empirical evidence from a number of large macroeconomic models that appears to be generally consistent with the views argued in the present chapter.[1]

GENERAL FRAMEWORK OF ANALYSIS

At the most general level, we need to have a framework for discussing macroeconomic policy that is broader than that normally employed. This is because the use of macroeconomic instruments to work towards the achievement of two or more macroeconomic objectives requires us to know at least the direction, and often also the relative extent, of the effect of a change of each instrument upon each macroeconomic objective. If it were really true that all instruments had the same effect on prices for a given effect on real output, those two macro objectives could not be pursued simultaneously – except in the trivial sense that a policy designed to have the desired effect on one of them might happen on some occasions also to have the desired effect on the other.

But if there are at least two macroeconomic instruments that have different effects on prices for a given effect on real output or employment, it becomes possible to adopt combinations of those measures that will work towards the achievement of both the desired level of real output and the desired rise in prices over the period towards which policy is being directed.

Unfortunately, the combinations of assumptions upon which such macroeconomic mixes are available are generally not considered by the more limited framework used for discussing and thinking about policy that is usually implicit (or even explicit) in the way in which macroeconomic policy discussions are conducted, and usually taught in economics courses.

For, at one extreme – which may be loosely described as 'Keynesian' – the emphasis generally placed upon the relationship between the level of activity (relative to full employment) and the rate of increase in prices, leads to the implicit assumption that the change in prices over a period will be affected *only* by the consideration of how close the economy is to full employment (perhaps together with the rate at which full employment is being approached), without due attention being paid also to the influence of the combination of macroeconomic instruments on the rate of increase in prices at any given level, or rate of increase, of real output or employment.

At the other extreme, the monetarist approach (which was very influential from about the mid-1970s to about the mid-1980s) inclined to the view that none of the macroeconomic instruments could have real effects, except that monetary expansion could temporarily raise real output or employment; and that an expansionary monetary policy, as measured by the rate of monetary growth would (alone among macroeconomic measures) eventually affect only inflation but not real output or employment.

Those two conflicting views (characterised here as the 'Keynesian' and the monetarist) – different though they were in so many respects from one another – shared the same characteristic that their assumptions left no scope for varying the combination of monetary policy with different fiscal measures in such a way as to have different *combinations* of effects on the two policy objectives (the level, or rate of growth, of real output or employment, on the one hand, and the rate of increase in prices over the period, on the other).

But many alternative combinations of assumptions can be made about the effects of different macroeconomic instruments upon the different objectives (many of them arguably more realistic than the two views outlined in the preceding paragraphs), on the basis of which there are combinations of measures that can be used to stimulate real output without increasing the upward pressure on prices (and, indeed, while simultaneously reducing it). Moreover, many of these combinations of assumptions are intermediate between the typically 'Keynesian' views and the typically monetarist ones – which makes it especially strange that a framework of analysis that is broad enough to encompass them has not become the basic paradigm within which macroeconomic policy is discussed.

One group of such assumptions would be if there is at least one instrument that reduces the upward pressure on prices while at the same time stimulating real output or employment. An example of this would be a form of tax cut that has such a large downward effect on costs or on money-wage demands as to exceed any upward pressure on prices that would otherwise result from the stimulus that it gives to demand.

A second group of such assumptions is where there are two or more macroeconomic instruments, each of which affects a different macro objective, but has no appreciable effect on the other objective. For example, monetary policy might eventually affect only prices (but not real output or employment), and tax cuts – of an appropriate sort – might affect only real output or employment (but not prices). Obviously, in that case each of these instruments could be directed towards dealing with the macroeconomic objective that it was able to influence, and the use of each of them to affect that objective would then have no undesired side-effects on the other. If these instruments were used in that way, it would involve using tax cuts to provide an expansionary effect, and tightening monetary policy to reduce inflation – an apparently contradictory combination of expansionary plus contractionary measures, which would be virtually ruled out by the conventional way of thinking, which, in this sense, virtually considers macroeconomic policy as a single instrument.

More generally, even if the available macroeconomic instruments all tend to exert upward pressure on prices in the process of providing a real stimulus, provided that they do not raise prices over the period of concern to the policy maker to the same extent for a given real stimulus, there is a combination of macroeconomic measures available that can raise real output and reduce the upward pressure on prices (or leave it unchanged). This can be done if the more inflationary of the two instruments is moved in a contractionary direction, and the less inflationary one in an expansionary direction on a sufficient scale to leave a net real stimulus but a downward (or zero) net effect on the increase in prices. (This policy, too, would appear to be paradoxical to the conventional way of thinking – as one policy measure would be moved in an expansionary direction and the other in a contractionary direction.)

At the most general level, we therefore need to ask what is the likely direction, and the relative extent, of the effects of each of the available macroeconomic instruments on each of the two main macroeconomic objectives. The three types of macroeconomic instruments are (i) changes in the setting of monetary policy, usually by way of operations by the central bank in the market for government securities, coupled with the decisions of the government about how far to finance a given budget deficit by the creation of money and how much by the sale of bonds (or how much of any surplus to use to redeem bonds, and how much to reduce monetary growth); (ii) changes in the level of government outlays; and (iii) changes in the general level of taxation.

There are a number of arguments that might be raised on *a priori* grounds about the direction and effect of each instrument upon each of the two main macroeconomic objectives.

Taking first an easing of monetary policy, it may be argued at one extreme that it may have all its effects on prices, rather than on real output, as it operates mainly (some might say, entirely) by temporarily raising the actual rate of increase in prices above what is expected; and that when expectations catch up with reality (which may be very quickly) the real stimulus will disappear; and may never occur at all if people come to expect the monetary stimulus and its consequences, and thus adjust their expectations even before it occurs.

On the other hand, it might also be argued that in some circumstances, especially when there are ample spare resources in an economy, a monetary expansion is likely to lead to a considerable rise in real output or employment, and that the consequent rise in real output will enable firms to operate at nearer to their optimum level of output or employment, and so help to hold down unit costs, and to that extent the prices of the finished products. In other words, it would be hard to rule out completely the possibility that even a monetary stimulus might in some circumstances lead to increases in real output or employment without upward pressure on prices. The hypothesis that monetary expansion might sometimes actually reduce prices without stimulating real output would, however, be the most difficult case to argue among the various hypothetical combinations of effects of different instruments that we are considering.

If we now consider tax cuts, there are clearly two conflicting effects (both on prices and on output). On the one hand, a tax cut (even a bond-financed tax cut) will have some effect in the direction of stimulating real output, provided that there are any spare resources in the economy, and that the sale of bonds to finance the tax cuts does not crowd out an amount of private spending at least as great as the stimulus to private spending resulting from the tax cuts. In theory, however, cases could arise where the crowding out effect of the bond sales could equal or even exceed the direct stimulatory effects of the tax cut – however unlikely this might seem to be in reality. In principle, therefore, the effect of tax cuts on real output or employment could be upward, downward, or neutral.

Tax cuts do not operate primarily (if at all) by raising the actual rate of increase in prices above that which producers expect, but rather by reducing the costs of producers, either directly through reducing the taxes they have to pay on their inputs or on the numbers they employ; or indirectly, by reducing the pre-tax incomes at which people are willing to offer goods or services, or to accept employment. The use of tax cuts as a stimulatory measure does not, therefore, suffer from the disadvantage of an expansionary monetary policy of relying for much (or even all) of its effectiveness on people's expectations about the rate of increase in prices lagging behind the actual rate. Of course, it is true that when the economy has fully adjusted to a tax cut one would not expect that tax cut to provide *further* stimulus; so that in *this sense* it is an *unexpected* tax cut that may be expected to have the real effect. It is also true that if people *expect* a fall in *income tax* rates some of the stimulus may occur before those taxes are actually cut; in that sense, it may be said that an unanticipated (income tax) cut is likely to be more effective in raising real output or employment *after* the tax cut; though the expectation of cuts in *indirect* tax rates works in the opposite direction – tending to make people postpone their purchases until the tax cut actually occurs.

The conclusion about the effects of tax cuts on real output or employment is thus that they will almost certainly be in an upward direction, unless the economy is very close to full employment, or the crowding out effects of the bond sales are very strong, or the effects of a tax cut (in the form of income tax cuts) have already been fully anticipated in people's spending decisions. At worst, one might thus expect the effect of a tax cut on real output to be negligible.

As to the price effects of tax cuts, there is, on the one hand, the upward effect on prices that the cuts will almost certainly have through the stimulus to the real level of demand (unless the economy starts from very high levels of unemployment), as the stimulus brings the economy closer to full employment. But, on the other hand, there is the downward effect on costs (and to that extent on prices at any given level of employment or real output) that results from cuts in taxes on the inputs and capital equipment that employers purchase; and from the tendency for money wage demands to be reduced (at any given level or rate of increase in employment) by cuts in taxes that affect wage and salary earners. It is an empirical matter which of these two effects on prices dominates the other, or whether they more or less offfset one another.[2] It could therefore be argued that tax cuts may either increase or reduce the upward pressure on prices, or that they may leave it about the same; and that the type of taxes that are cut may well have an important influence on both the direction and extent of this outcome.

Finally, if we consider the effects of (bond-financed) government outlays on the two main macroeconomic objectives, one might argue that their effects on real output could be either upward or downward (or negligible) – according to the strength of any crowding-out effect of the bond sales upon private expenditure, and on whether the outlays by the government replace private spending that people would otherwise have felt it necessary to undertake themselves. Their effects on prices can similarly be a subject of dispute – for some government outlays may help to hold down business costs, either by subsidising their inputs (and perhaps even their wage and salary costs or their costs of training labour); and may do so indirectly if they result in better roads and ports or other facilities that increase productive efficiency in bringing the goods to market.

On the other hand, government outlays may absorb resources that could otherwise have been used in private production for the market, and may use those resources less efficiently than the private sector; and, if so, the net effect of the government outlays on prices is especially likely to be upward, for any given level of employment.

We have therefore raised (at the most general level) in the preceding paragraphs, some arguments about the possible direction of the effects of each of the main groups of macroeconomic instruments on each of the main macro objectives; and suggested circumstances in which those effects might be in one direction or the other – and thus that those opposing effects might cancel one another out, leading to the further possibility that the effect of any of these instruments on either of the objectives might in some circumstances be negligible.

A framework for considering macroeconomic policy that allows for the possibility of any combinations of these effects seems therefore to be needed.

We turn now to consider more specific arguments relating to the most likely direction and relative extent of the effects of each of these instruments on each of the main objectives; and so to the question of what combinations of assumptions about those effects are most likely to be valid.

MONETARY POLICY

The first argument is that a relatively expansionary monetary policy (with an unchanged setting of fiscal instruments) will have a greater upward effect on prices for a given real stimulus than if either of the fiscal instruments had been employed to provide the stimulus; indeed, in an extreme case, and after a few years, it is likely that all the impact of a move towards a more expansionary monetary policy will be on the price level rather than on real output or employment.

This may be partly by reason of expectational effects: people may believe that an expansionary policy is more inflationary than any form of fiscal stimulus, and to that extent an easing of monetary policy is likely to be more inflationary than other forms of stimulus having the same effect on real output. A monetarist view would be consistent with this approach: an expansionary monetary policy raises real output or employment only so long as it raises the actual inflation rate above that which people expect. When expectations catch up with the actual rate of inflation, however, this real stimulus wears off – money wage rates catching up with prices and leaving businesses no longer willing to provide more employment. But it is also consistent with a less extreme view; namely, that some of the real stimulus provided by a monetary expansion continues (perhaps indefinitely), but that it is accompanied by a greater rise in prices over the relevant period than would have resulted from a fiscal stimulus having the same effect on real output.

It may also be argued that, as an expansionary monetary policy operates by reducing the real post-tax return on financial assets (at least in the short run), this is likely to have the effect of inducing holders of financial assets to shift toward holding relatively more of certain types of real assets – gold, real estate, commodities, precious stones and so on – that are durable substitutes for financial assets. As these tend to be products that are in relatively inelastic supply, this leads to upward pressure on the general price level – as the output of newly produced commodities of this sort is gradually increased to meet part of the extra demand for them. But as the supply of such goods is inherently less responsive than that of commodities in general to a rise in the demand for them (indeed, this is probably the main reason why they are regarded as good alternatives to financial assets), this results in a *general* rise in the price level.[3]

This same argument may help to explain why a cut in interest rates tends to make the owners of exhaustible resources keep them in the ground (or demand higher prices for them) to a greater extent than they would at the same general level of activity if there were higher real post-tax interest rates. This upward pressure on the prices of exhaustible resources such as minerals and fuel may well (as the oil price booms of the 1970s showed) have macroeconomic effects in the form of rising prices generally at any given level, or rate of increase, of general economic activity – at least if accompanied by an accommodating monetary policy.

One might perhaps have argued – prior to the experience of the oil booms of the 1970s – that upward pressure on the price of oil would not have an effect on prices in general: but so long as other prices – most notably money wage rates – are not on the average as flexible downwards as those of oil (and perhaps other important commodities) are flexible upwards in such situations, the net effect of upward pressure on the general price level, such as occurred in 1973–74 and 1979–80, is not at all surprising. On the other hand, it is reasonable to argue that without expansionary monetary policies such as those of the early 1970s the oil price rises would not have had so much upward effect on prices – though they might then have had *different* macroeconomic effects, in the form of a greater downward effect on real output and employment.

TAX CUTS AND GOVERNMENT OUTLAYS

The second set of arguments about the relative effects of alternative forms of macroeconomic stimulus relates to tax cuts as a stimulatory measure. The presumption must be that these have less tendency to raise prices (or a greater tendency to reduce prices) at any given level or rate of increase of real output than either an easing of monetary policy (for the reasons relating to monetary policy argued above) or an increase in government spending (for reasons argued below).

The principal reason for this is that tax increases or tax cuts are likely to have some direct effects on the cost structure of businesses, and to that extent on the prices that businesses require to persuade them to produce a given output. This is easy to see if the businesses are paying payroll tax (or national insurance contributions in the UK, or social security contributions in Continental Europe) on their employees, or indirect taxes on the fuel they use. When these taxes are cut, it is therefore likely that this will lead to a reduction in the price level, even when it results also in a rise in employment or real output; but, at the very least, it is likely to mean that tax cuts of this sort are likely to have less upward effect (if any) on the price level than are government outlays of the same order, which will normally have no such cost-reducing effect unless they consist of direct subsidies on the costs of businesses.

Cuts in indirect taxes are likely to make wage-earners willing to accept lower pre-tax money wage increases than they would if these taxes were higher: for (to some greater or smaller extent) wage and salary earners are interested in their real post-tax income – rather than merely in what they earn pre-tax.

This is also true of the direct taxes (income taxes) imposed on wage and salary earners. Where the taxes imposed on them, especially the marginal income taxes, are high, they are likely to demand bigger increases in their pre-tax incomes than when marginal income tax is lower. This is especially likely to be a relevant factor in countries where marginal income tax rates on the typical wage-earner are relatively high. It is therefore a consideration that has become of importance in many countries over the course of the 1960s and 1970s, and in some (but not all) countries has probably fallen in significance as the higher marginal rates of income tax have been reduced during the 1980s. One would not argue on *a priori* grounds that cuts in income tax are likely both to raise employment and reduce prices (as one may certainly argue could be true for cuts in indirect taxes and in payroll taxes such as employers' social security contributions). But cuts in income taxes are likely to lead to *less upward* pressure on prices for a given stimulus to real output or employment than is the typical rise in government outlays.

This may not be true, however, in respect of some forms of government outlay. At one extreme there may be forms of government subsidy that operate very like tax cuts to hold down costs, prices and money wage rates. Some forms of government outlay (usually among those that governments are most likely to cut, as being politically less sensitive) may also tend to hold up productivity and to hold down the retail prices of goods – notably the provision of better roads and ports.

But these are not the typical form of government outlay. It may be that there is some presumption that government outlays on capital projects (and, indeed, government outlays generally) are not generally as well calculated to raise productivity as are most investment outlays by private businesses – if only because government outlays are more likely to be aimed at maximising votes, or perhaps at furthering the interests of the policy makers or their advisers, than at raising real output per person or per unit of capital.

Without necessarily accepting that view, however, one may argue that there is a reasonable presumption that government outlays are not so likely (for the reasons outlined above relating to money wage demands and the prices charged by businesses on whom taxes are levied) to help restrain the rise in prices at any given level or rate of increase in employment or real output as are most types of tax cut (even assuming that either fiscal measure has the same effect on productivity).

One qualification that ought to be made to this statement is that certain types of government social expenditures may in some countries constitute part of an (implicit or explicit) arrangement with the unions to limit their wage demands. Just as there may be 'wage-tax trade-offs', so there may also be 'wage-government social spending trade offs'. In principle, if unions attached more weight to the maintenance or increase of such social expenditures than to reductions in the taxes on their incomes, or on the goods and services their members purchase, they might even be more willing to observe restraint in their wage demands in response to undertakings by the government to raise its outlays on certain forms of social expenditure than in response to tax cuts.

But, in fact, the average union member (and presumably his or her union leaders) is likely to attach more weight to money in the pay-packet than to social expenditure (from which he or she may or may not benefit). Moreover, even if every trade unionist or other employee were convinced that they would benefit from these social expenditures, there would always be the 'free-rider' problem – for the benefit derived by the individual from these outlays is in no way related to his or her (pre-tax or post-tax) wages: each individual would thus probably be more likely to accept the benefit of these expenditures without reducing wage demands than if the benefit offered by the government in return for wage restraint was a rise in post-tax income. It may be difficult to rationalise this assertion; but it would seem intuitively likely to be true – if only because the wage or salary earner can see the extra money in the pay-packet that results from a wage-tax trade-off, but can see only the *lower* post-tax money wage that results from a trade-off of wage restraint against a higher level of government outlays.

In any case, even in the absence of explicit trade-offs between government and unions about wage restraint in return for expansionary fiscal measures of either sort, the presumption must be that tax cuts have some effect in restraining pre-tax wage demands, as post-tax wages will then (in real terms) be greater than in the absence of the tax cuts if those reduce either the direct taxes paid by the wage or salary earner or the prices of the products purchased with those wages or salaries. There is clearly not normally a comparable upward effect on the purchasing power of a given level of (nominal) pre-tax wages when there is a rise in government outlays (rather than a cut in tax rates).

The presumption ought, therefore, to be that a bond-financed tax cut would exert less upward (or a greater downward) effect on prices than would a bond-financed rise in the typical form of government outlay, for any given real stimulus to output or employment: and that either fiscal measure would be likely to exert less upward pressure on prices (again for a given real stimulus) than would an expansionary monetary policy.

We have so far considered pure fiscal measures; that is to say, ones that are financed by the sale of bonds to the public, rather than being accompanied by any easing of monetary policy to hold interest rates down in the face of the fiscal expansion.

If the alternatives being considered include also a rise in government spending that is financed by creating money (on a scale sufficient to prevent interest rates from rising), this is clearly in principle a form of stimulus that is intermediate between a pure monetary expansion and a pure (bond-financed) rise in government outlays. The accommodating stance of monetary policy in this case makes it less likely that government outlays will 'crowd out' private spending through upward pressure on interest rates than with a bond-financed rise in government outlays, but, because of the absence of that upward effect on interest rates, there would be a greater upward effect on prices, for any given rise in government outlays, when there is an accommodating monetary policy to hold interest rates down (for reasons discussed above, pp. 11–13).

It is thus difficult to be sure *a priori* whether the upward pressure on prices with this accommodated rise in government outlays will be greater (for a given rise in real output or employment) than with a bond-financed rise in government outlays. For, on the one hand, one would expect that the accommodating monetary policy, to hold down interest rates, would be more likely to exert upward pressure on prices, for the same reasons as were argued above in relation to an expansionary monetary policy; but, on the other hand, there will be a greater stimulus to real output or employment, for a given rise in government outlays, than if the government outlays had been bond-financed, and has thus been more likely to crowd out private spending. Similar arguments might be raised about tax cuts financed by the creation of money on a scale sufficient to hold down interest rates in the face of the tax cuts. As tax cuts operate solely by encouraging private expenditure, however, they are less likely than are government outlays to 'crowd out' (other) private spending to a fully offsetting extent, even if they are bond financed.

One could thus expect that tax cuts, with an accommodating monetary policy, would have a greater upward effect on real output than would a similarly accommodated rise in government outlays of the same order of magnitude.

In some cases, a change in a single instrument can contribute to both objectives – stimulating real output or employment while *reducing* prices. This is most likely to be true of cuts in indirect taxes and of cuts in payroll taxes, such as employers' social security or national insurance contributions, as we shall from the empirical evidence in Chapter 3. But even if all the available forms of macroeconomic stimulus raised prices in the process of increasing real output or employment, it would not be true that stimulatory policies would inevitably tend to raise prices – provided that there are at least two instruments with different effects on prices for a given effect on real output or employment.

THE USE OF TWO OR MORE INSTRUMENTS

If a government has the aim of reducing the upward pressure on prices, and sustaining or increasing the growth of real output or reducing unemployment, it can adopt a combination of measures that will do this provided that at least two of the available instruments do not have exactly the same effect on prices for a given effect on output or employment. (This assumes, of course, that there are at least two instruments that can be changed independently.)

For example, if a government has only the two instruments of tax rates and monetary policy – that is, assuming, for the purposes of illustration, that it is unable or unwilling to change the level of government outlays – it can still change the setting of those two available instruments in such a way as to stimulate growth without increasing inflation (or, on slightly more exacting conditions, to reduce both the upward pressure on prices and the level of unemployment) on certain conditions.

Clearly, if monetary policy affected only prices, whereas tax rates (without any accompanying change in monetary policy) affected only real output or employment, an ideal situation would exist; for each instrument could then be moved in the appropriate direction to deal with the macroeconomic objective on which it had a helpful effect, and there would then be no unwanted side-effects from the use of each of those instruments to deal with the objective to which it was suited. Of course, if the two instruments were moved in the *wrong* direction – higher tax rates being used to try to hold down inflation, and monetary expansion to try to stimulate real output – that combination of measures would, on the stated assumptions, have adverse effects on both macroeconomic objectives, and no helpful effects at all.

Very similar conclusions would follow if one of the instruments had an insignificant effect on one of the objectives – for example, if monetary expansion had little lasting effect on real output – whereas the other instrument (tax cuts in this case) affected both real output and prices. In this case it is clearly important to move monetary policy in the appropriate direction to have the desired downward effect on the price level (the only objective on which it has a significant effect in this case), and to use tax cuts to deal with unemployment. Again, if a government was in this case unwise enough to try to use monetary expansion to deal with unemployment it could only make inflation worse; and if it then tried to deal with the resulting inflation by raising tax rates it would also make unemployment worse (even though the tax increase would have some effect in restraining price increases). This case therefore illustrates especially clearly that it would be essential to choose the direction for the change of setting of each of the instruments that was appropriate for dealing with this situation in the light of the effects, if any, of *each* of the instruments on *each* objective.

The policy implications would be much the same in the much more likely situation where both tax cuts and monetary expansion have *some* upward effect on both prices and output (or employment), but where monetary expansion has a relatively greater upward effect on prices than do tax cuts, for a given stimulus to real output. For in this case also, if monetary expansion is used in the hope of stimulating output or employment, and if taxes are raised in the hope of curbing inflation, this combination of measures will drive the economy further away from both of its desired goals of holding down inflation and reducing unemployment.

CONCLUSIONS

The argument of this chapter has been that the various macroeconomic instruments should not be assumed to have identical effects on prices for a given effect in stimulating real output or employment; for there are good *a priori* reasons to suppose that this is not so. In some circumstances the effect of each of the instruments on prices or real output might (alternatively) be either upward, downward or negligible; and the precise combinations of the direction and extent of the effect on prices for a given real stimulus will have an important bearing on the choice of combinations of instruments that ought to be employed in order to have any desired effect on real output (or employment) and prices over the period for which a government is formulating its policy.

Moreover, it is not sufficient to think of macroeconomic policy merely in terms of monetary policy on the one hand and fiscal policy on the other; for there may be important differences between government outlays and tax cuts, and also between cuts in one type of tax and cuts in another, in terms of the extent, and even the direction, in which changes in the various taxes affect prices (for a given effect on real output or employment).

The *a priori* arguments of this chapter have, however, suggested that, of the principal macroeconomic instruments, an easing of monetary policy is likely to have a greater upward effect on prices than the typical form of government outlay (for a given real stimulus); and that tax cuts are likely to have the least upward effect on prices, while some types of tax cut may even exert downward pressure on prices in the process of stimulating real output or employment.

Finally, provided that there are even two macroeconomic instruments that have different effects on prices for a given real stimulus, and even if both instruments tend to increase the upward pressure on prices when they are used to raise real output or employment, there is a combination of the two that can provide a non-inflationary (indeed, price-reducing) real stimulus, if the more inflationary of the two is moved in a contractionary direction and the less inflationary of the two in an expansionary direction to an appropriate extent. These propositions will be illustrated in Chapter 4 after empirical evidence has been assembled in Chapter 3 about the relative effects of different macroeconomic instruments on prices for a given effect on real output or employment.

NOTES

1. Most of these arguments have been put forward in greater detail by the present author in earlier books. (See Perkins 1979, 1982 and 1985.)
2. The second of these two effects may be depicted as a rightward shift of the aggregate supply schedule – which relates employment on the horizontal axis to prices on the vertical axis – indicating that a higher level of employment will be offered at any given level of prices. This shift may exceed or fall short of (or, of course, it might just offset) the rightward shift of the aggregate demand schedule that results from the tax cuts.
3. See Lindbeck, 1979 and Perkins, 1986.

3 Internal Objectives: Empirical Evidence

This chapter assembles empirical evidence from a number of sources that throws light on the probable validity of the hypotheses raised in Chapter 2: namely, that different forms of macroeconomic stimulus have different relative effects on prices for a given effect on real output or employment; in particular, that tax cuts are likely to have less upward effect on prices than government outlays (and some types of tax cut may even have a downward effect on prices) for any given real stimulus to output or employment, and that a monetary expansion is likely to have the greatest upward effect on prices for any given real stimulus.

It should be borne in mind that the results of simulations with any particular econometric model clearly depend on the characteristics of that model, and that other models may give different results – which are in any event subject to wide margins of error, which may be still greater if one uses simulations of different instruments (even from the same econometric model) to derive a conclusion about the probable effects of changing both those instruments simultaneously.

The use made of these results for the purpose of discussion of policy issues relates, however, primarily to the direction and the ranking of the effects of the various instruments on the different objectives; and the precise numerical value of these effects is not intended to be used for drawing any more exact conclusions. But it appears permissible to use these results partly as an illustration of the principles involved, and also to suggest conclusions about the directions of change in the various instruments that are most likely to contribute towards dealing with a given combination of macroeconomic problems.

In this sense, the policy implications of the results from the various models used in this chapter are consistent with one another to a remarkable extent (as the summary of conclusions from this evidence, at the end of this chapter, makes clear), and are also generally consistent with the *a priori* arguments given in Chapter 2 about the direction and ranking of the effects of the various instruments on the different objectives discussed. We shall, however, discuss in Chapter 4 not only the implications of simplified versions of the empirical results in this chapter, but also those of various alternative combinations of assumptions;

for it is probable that different models and additional evidence will suggest that there are other combinations of assumptions that may be more likely to be valid for particular countries and particular periods. At the very least, the results derived in the present chapter can serve to illustrate the principles that should be applied – on given assumptions about the relative effects of different instruments – in choosing combinations of macroeconomic measures to raise output or employment with minimal upward effect on prices, and even with a downward effect on prices.

The first and most important conclusion is that, for every country, each of the various measures simulated has different relative effects on prices for a given effect on real output. Considerations of comparative advantage are therefore, on this evidence, relevant and applicable in determining appropriate macroeconomic policies in situations where the aim is to raise real output without increasing prices (or, preferably, while reducing them). On this evidence, therefore, it would not be rational to resist the taking of some expansionary measure merely because of a fear that *any* form of expansion must tend to raise prices: for there are (on the basis of the arguments given in Chapter 2) *combinations* of two (or more) of these three measures that would, on this evidence, both raise real output and reduce prices, even when (as in the cases which are covered in the OECD simulations) any one of the measures individually would raise prices in the process of raising real output.

The second important conclusion is that, taking the upward pressure on the level of prices over the average of the five years, the hierarchy of these measures is (with the partial exception of Canada) that suggested in Chapter 2 as being the most likely on *a priori* grounds. That is, compared with either form of bond-financed fiscal stimulus, the monetary measure of expansion (in this case a reduction of two percentage points in short-term interest rates), is the most 'inflationary' – in the sense that it exerts greatest upward pressure on the average price level over the period in question for a given real stimulus; while bond-financed income tax cuts are the least inflationary of these three measures, with bond-financed government outlays being intermediate in terms of their effects on the average price level during the period for a given stimulus to real output (see Table 3.1). The partial exception to this generalisation among the seven countries is that for Canada the simulations suggest that government outlays are the most inflationary and a reduction in short-term interest rates the *least* inflationary of the three instruments, with income tax cuts being intermediate between

Table 3.1 Effects on prices of alternative measures for 1 per cent stimulus to real GDP/GNP with floating exchange rates, seven major OECD countries (Change in annual average level compared with base over five years, with average annual rise over the period in parentheses) (per cent)

	US	*Japan*	*West Germany*	*France*	*UK*	*Italy*	*Canada*
Income tax cut (money constant)	*1.65* (0.77)	*0.52* (0.80)	*0.29* (*0.07*)	*0.18* (*0.07*)	*0.24* (0.15)	*0.34* (0.20)	1.71 (1.60)
Income tax cut (interest rates constant)	1.18 (*0.64*)	0.57 (*0.26*)	0.82 (0.27)	0.40 (0.12)	1.60 (0.68)	0.59 (0.32)	1.47 (*0.58*)
Rise in government outlays (money constant)	2.30 (1.35)	0.63 *	0.40 (0.50)	0.29 (0.08)	0.48 (0.33)	0.51 (0.33)	2.41 *
Rise in government outlays (interest rates constant)	2.20 (0.87)	0.66 (0.32)	0.93 (0.40)	0.60 (0.21)	2.08 (0.91)	0.83 (0.45)	1.83 (0.90)
Cut in short-term interest rates	2.52 (0.95)	0.73 (0.22)	1.46 (0.40)	1.56 (0.33)	3.70 (1.09)	3.33 (0.77)	*1.30* (*0.43*)

* Indicates that this figure is undefined, the measure in question having no upward effect on real GDP by the end of the five years. The measure in question is thus on this measure more 'inflationary' than any of the others.
NOTE: The figures in italics show the least inflationary form of stimulus (on each of these two statistical measurements) for each country.
SOURCE: Data for rise in government outlays and cut in interest rates derived from Richardson, 1987 and 1988; results for income tax cuts derived from data supplied by Pete Richardson.

those other two instruments. But, for Canada, as for the others, an income tax cut is on these results less inflationary than a rise in government outlays.

We may also consider the relative effects of the alternative measures on the average annual *change* in prices for a given average annual stimulus of one per cent in GDP over a five-year period. On this criterion also a monetary stimulus is the most inflationary, except for Japan (for which it is the least inflationary of the measures tested), West Germany, for which on this criterion it is the second most inflationary, and Canada, for which the monetary expansion is again the least inflationary.

Bond-financed income tax cuts score better than bond-financed rises in government outlays for all seven countries; and (except for Canada, again, and the US) bond-financed tax cuts or bond-financed government outlays each score better than the same measure when it is accommodated by monetary measures to hold down interest rates, using the comparison of the effects over the average level for the five years. For the average annual change over the five-year period, however, the bond-financed alternatives are the more inflationary for the US, Japan and (for outlays) West Germany, as well as for Canada.

In short, in deciding what combination of measures to use to provide a non-inflationary stimulus, a government may have to decide whether it is more interested in the effect on the *average* of prices over the next five years, or whether it is more interested in the average annual *change* in prices over the whole period from the time the measures are introduced to the last of those years.

On either criterion, however, the prescription of tight monetary policy and bond-financed income tax cuts holds good for all countries except Canada (for which it did not hold for the average of the five years or the annual change over the period), and Japan for the change.

A rise in interest rates coupled with one of the forms of fiscal expansion would also, on this evidence, provide a non-inflationary (or price-reducing) stimulus in terms of the average level of prices over the five years, except for the US – for which that would not be true of an accommodated income tax cut. If the end of the period is the main consideration, this prescription would hold good for the US with income tax cuts, whether interest rates or the quantity of money is held constant, but with increases in government outlays it holds good only if interest rates are kept constant: but it would hold good for West Germany only with tax cuts, and not at all for Japan.

The prescription of simultaneously cutting government outlays and income tax rates, with money held constant, holds good, however, for all seven countries and irrespective of whether one is most interested in the effect over the average of the five years or the effect at the end of the period, and whether the interest rates or the quantity of money is held constant except for outlays in the US, on one measure.

Whether one is concerned mainly about the five-year average or about the change by the end of the period, one could – on this evidence – therefore prescribe some form of monetary restraint with one or more of these two types of fiscal expansion for all these countries except Canada, but for West Germany the tight monetary policy would best be combined with income tax cuts; while for the US the choice would depend partly on whether the main concern is with the end of the period or the average annual level.

INTERLINKED SIMULATION

For a rise in government outlays there is also available an interlinked simulation, which assesses the total effects of the measures after allowing for feedback effects from other countries on to the country adopting the measure. (See Richardson, 1987 and 1988.) For five of the countries this simulation does not appear to change appreciably the effect of government outlays on prices for a given effect on output. But for Japan and the US the upward effect on prices of a rise in government outlays (for a given effect on real output) is greater than in the simple model for those individual countries. Simulations for income tax cuts are not available for the interlinked model, and the results from a simulation with that model of a cut in short-term interest rates are not available on an exactly comparable basis to that for changes in government outlays. It is not, therefore, possible to say whether the relative ranking of the three instruments would be different if the results of an interlinked simulation were available for all of the three measures. The presumption would be, however, that for the US these feedback effects might be of importance, and perhaps to a lesser extent also for Japan, but for the other countries there is no reason to expect that they would substantially change the conclusions suggested by the models for the individual countries.

EFFECTS ON EMPLOYMENT AND PRICES

The OECD simulations can also be used to derive the effect of the alternative measures on prices for a given effect on *employment* (rather than real GDP). As Table 3.2 shows, much the same conclusions follow: that of the five measures simulated, and for five of the seven countries,

Table 3.2 Effect on prices of alternative measures for 1 per cent stimulus to employment with floating exchange rates, seven major OECD countries (change in annual average level compared with base over five years, with average annual change in parentheses) (per cent)

	US	*Japan*	*West Germany*	*France*	*UK*	*Italy*	*Canada*
Income tax cut (money constant)	3.59 (2.30)	*2.43* (1.60)	*0.67* (0.13)	*0.64* (0.20)	*0.35* (0.20)	*1.62* (0.70)	*2.77* (1.20)
Income tax cut (interest rate constant)	*3.26* (1.13)	3.49 (0.93)	1.07 (0.23)	1.46 (0.40)	2.57 (0.97)	3.57 (1.30)	2.52 (1.30)
Rise in government outlays (money constant)	5.85 (*)	2.75 (1.80)	0.82 (0.20)	0.76 (0.24)	0.57 (0.21)	2.33 (1.00)	3.42 (*)
Rise in government outlays (interest rates constant)	4.21 (1.74)	3.11 (1.16)	1.08 (0.25)	1.89 (0.57)	3.06 (1.25)	4.44 (1.80)	3.13 (2.25)
Cut in short-term interest rates	3.61 (1.52)	3.75 (0.93)	1.17 (0.22)	8.33 (2.00)	6.54 (1.90)	* (*)	3.25 (1.30)

* Signifies that there is no rise in employment over the period as a whole for these countries, so that this figure is undefined, making it the most inflationary of the measures tested.
NOTE: The figures in italics show the least inflationary form of stimulus for each country in the period in question.
SOURCE: as for Table 3.1.

monetary expansion clearly has the greatest upward effect on prices for a given effect on employment over the average of the succeeding five years; and for five of the countries a bond-financed cut in income taxes clearly has the least inflationary effect, with bond-financed government outlays being intermediate betweem the two other forms of stimulus.

For Canada, these results (like those in Table 3.1) suggest that a monetary expansion is the one with *least* upward effect on the average level of prices over the five years; but for that country, as for all the other countries, income tax cuts are in this sense less inflationary than are increases in government outlays financed in the same way. An important exception to the general ranking is that (in contrast to Table 3.1) for the US a monetary expansion appears to be *less* inflationary for a given effect on employment than government outlays with interest rates or money held constant.

If the criterion is the effect on prices for a given effect on *unemployment* (rather than *employment*), the conclusion from these simulations (details of which are not included here) is that a cut in income tax scores better than a rise in government outlays for all countries; and the margin of the comparative advantage of income tax cuts over increases in government outlays is greater on this criterion than for *employment* for all countries other than the US.

It is not necessarily surprising that for some countries the accommodated form of fiscal expansion (with monetary policy changed in such a way as to hold interest rates constant) is less inflationary for a given real stimulus than a bond-financed fiscal stimulus. For it may be remembered that it was pointed out in Chapter 2 that a fiscal stimulus that is accompanied by an accommodating monetary policy, to hold interest rates constant, does not have an unambiguous ranking (relative to the bond-financed alternative) in terms of the *a priori* arguments raised in that chapter. For, on the one hand, the accommodation of a fiscal expansion by an easing of monetary policy makes the fiscal expansion less likely to 'crowd out' various forms of private spending, so that the upward effect on real output or employment may be expected to be correspondingly greater than with the bond-financed alternative; but, on the other hand, the monetary expansion itself (to hold down interest rates in the face of the fiscal stimulus) may be expected to have an upward effect on prices (at any given level or rate of increase in real output or employment) in addition to that which would be present with the bond-financed alternative. The net effect of these two considerations is thus ambiguous *a priori*.

It is therefore of interest to note that, as Tables 3.1 and 3.2 also show, in two of the countries covered – the US and Canada – the effect on the average level of prices over the five-year period of the accommodated form of both types of fiscal stimulus tested (for a given effect on output) is less than is the bond-financed alternative. For the rest of the countries the accommodated form of a fiscal stimulus exerts more upward pressure on prices over the course of the period than when the same form of fiscal stimulus is financed by bond sales (that is, with the quantity of money held constant). But for all countries (including the US and Canada), income tax cuts score more highly than does a rise in government outlays (in terms of minimising the rise in prices for a given real stimulus) if both these forms of fiscal stimulus are financed in the same way – that is, if interest rates are held constant by an accommodating monetary policy, or when each of them is assumed to be financed by the sale of bonds.

Even if a fiscal stimulus is accommodated, however, it appears on this evidence to be less inflationary than a cut in interest rates, for all the countries covered except Canada and the US. For Canada, both forms of fiscal stimulus, whether accommodated or not, are on this evidence more inflationary than a cut in short-term interest rates; while for the US an accommodated rise in government outlays is inferior on this score to a cut in interest rates, for a given effect on employment (though not for real output); and an accommodated cut in income tax rates has a more inflationary effect than a cut in short-term interest rates for any given stimulus to real output.

Taken as a whole, then, these OECD simulations constitute very compelling evidence for the view that the dichotomy of 'fiscal versus monetary' policy may be misleading and even dangerous. For, on this evidence, the two fiscal measures tested – income tax cuts and increases in government outlays – have different effects on prices for a given effect on output or employment; and the overwhelming balance of this evidence attests the superiority of income tax cuts over government outlays from this macroeconomic viewpoint. We shall see, on the basis of the results of other simulations reported below, that income tax cuts are much closer in their relative effects on prices to rises in government outlays than are other types of tax cuts – which might on that score be therefore expected to be even more markedly superior to government outlays than are cuts in income tax if the aim is to give a real stimulus with as little upward effect as possible on prices. But the policy prescriptions may vary in certain respects from one country to another.

In particular, although monetary expansion appears for most countries to be more inflationary than either of the two fiscal measures tested, it seems likely, on this evidence, that for the US and Canada monetary expansion may be *less* inflationary than a rise in government outlays or an income tax cut; but that tax cuts are likely to be preferable to increases in government outlays for those countries, as well as the others.

SIMULATIONS WITH MODELS OF THE UK ECONOMY

An extensive set of simulations for an individual country – which compares the simulated effects of a number of alternative macroeconomic stimuli by the use of all the major available econometric models for that country – are those undertaken for UK at the University of Warwick.[1]

As Tables 3.3 and 3.4 show, both the average for all the four quarterly models for which simulations of all the measures covered in these tests are available and also the ranking of the measures tested in three of the individual models provide strong evidence that cuts in the value-added tax (VAT) score especially highly. Indeed, in three of the models cuts in VAT not only stimulate output but (even though they are accompanied by a monetary policy that holds interest rates constant) also tend to reduce prices, a result that is confirmed by the simulations for the EEC reported below (which, in contrast to the simulations for

Table 3.3 Effects on prices of alternative measures for 1 per cent stimulus to real GDP in the UK (change in average annual level over first five years after the stimulus) (per cent)

Stimulus *Model*	*LBS*	*NIESR*	*HMT*	*B of E*	*Average of the four models*
Cut in VAT*	1.49	−0.82	−2.48	−3.91	−1.43
Cut in employers' national insurance contributions*	10.88	−0.88	−1.64	−2.03	1.58
Cut in income tax rates*	2.76	1.37	0.53	−1.82	0.71
Rise in government outlays*	1.40	1.23	1.98	1.05	1.41
Rise in government outlays (money constant)	0.38	1.14	7.69	1.03	2.56
Cut in short-term interest rates	2.33	1.09	1.23	2.08	1.68

* Signifies that the fiscal change is accommodated by monetary measures to hold interest rates constant.
SOURCE: Derived from Fisher *et al*, 1988.
LBS = London Business School; NIESR = National Institute of Economic and Social Research; HMT = Her Majesty's Treasury; B of E = Bank of England.

Table 3.4 Effects on consumer prices of alternative measures for rise in employment of 100 000 in the UK (average annual rise over five years) (per cent)

Stimulus *Model*	*LBS*	*NIESR*	*HMT*	*B of E*	*Average of the four models*
Cut in VAT*	0.54	−0.27	−1.16	−1.85	−0.69
Cut in employers' national insurance contributions	1.05	−0.38	−0.66	−1.04	−0.26
Cut in income tax*	1.80	0.52	0.30	−1.02	−0.40
Rise in government outlays*	0.73	0.40	0.60	0.35	0.52
Rise in government outlays (money constant)	0.14	0.44	0.54	0.35	0.37
Cut in interest rates	1.14	0.48	0.42	0.92	0.74

* Signifies that the fiscal stimulus in question is accommodated by monetary measures to hold interest rates constant.
SOURCE: Derived from Fisher *et al.*, 1988.

the UK, assume a constant quantity of money). The simulations of cuts in employers' national insurance contributions provide evidence from three of the models that this form of stimulus also operates in a helpful direction on both of the main macroeconomic objectives (in one of them even better than a cut in VAT) – a conclusion that we shall see below is also consistent with the EEC simulations. In one model income tax cuts also reduce prices.

When the fiscal stimuli are both accommodated by a sufficiently expansionary monetary policy to hold interest rates constant, the evidence from the UK models is mixed on whether government outlays are more inflationary than income tax cuts; though on the average of the models these results are consistent with the results from the OECD simulations to the effect that the income tax cut is the less inflationary of the two.

The ranking of the various policy shocks as indicated by the averages for the four models in Table 3.4 – though not the ranking in Table 3.3 – is consistent with the ranking of those measures tested also in the OECD simulations; interest rate cuts being the most inflationary, followed by accommodated government outlays, then bond-financed government outlays. Income tax cuts are generally more inflationary than the other tax cuts. The averages in Table 3.4 (but only to a limited extent those in Table 3.3), are also consistent with the EEC simulations reported below, so far as there are policy measures common to both; for in the EEC simulations also cuts in indirect taxes and employers' social security contributions had downward effects on prices, and income tax cuts had a less inflationary effect than government outlays.

In summary, then, this extensive evidence for the UK suggests that, if the aim is to provide a non-inflationary stimulus, cuts in VAT are the best, together with cuts in employers' national insurance contributions, even though both are assumed in these tests to be accompanied by an accommodating monetary policy. The ranking of the other expansionary measures simulated in these tests differs from one model to another; and of those that are also covered in the OECD simulations, only the Bank of England model would give the same ranking in terms of their effects on prices for a given effect on real output (shown in Table 3.3) as the OECD results reported above; though their ranking in terms of their effects on prices for a given effect on employment (shown in Table 3.4) is consistent with the ranking in the OECD results.

SIMULATIONS FOR THE EEC

Simulations undertaken by the staff of the European Commission[2] relate to the effects of alternative forms of (bond-financed) fiscal stimulus, but do not include the alternative of monetary expansion (see Table 3.5). Only one of them, that for the rise in government outlays, is therefore broadly comparable to one of those reported above as being undertaken with the UK econometric models; and only those for (bond-financed) income tax cuts and those for rises in government outlays are directly comparable to simulations by the OECD. They are, however, interesting and helpful as broadly confirming most of the evidence for the UK (discussed above) relating to the ranking of different types of tax cut (even though the EEC simulations assume the cuts are bond financed, whereas the UK simulations assumed that they were accommodated).

The main respect in which these results confirm the balance of the evidence from those for the UK is that cuts in VAT and reductions in employers' social security/national insurance contributions have a helpful effect on *both* objectives – tending to stimulate growth and

Table 3.5 Effects of alternative fiscal stimuli equal to 1 per cent of GDP on real GDP and prices in the EEC (effect on average annual level over five years as per cent of base)

	Effect on real GDP	*Effect on GDP price index*
Rise in public investment	0.88	0.88
Cut in household direct taxes	0.60	0.48
Cut in indirect taxes	1.02	–1.20
Cut in employers' social security contributions	0.90	–1.04

SOURCE: Derived from Dramais, 1986.

employment, as well as exerting downward pressure on prices. Moreover, the comparison between government outlays and income tax cuts gives a result that is consistent with those of the OECD simulations; for the EEC results imply that, for a given real stimulus, income tax cuts are less inflationary than a general rise in government outlays (as Table 3.6 shows).

As Table 3.6 shows, these results imply that there are various cuts in the different types of taxes simulated that could be combined with a cut in government outlays to give a non-inflationary stimulus.

Table 3.6 Change in tax rates to give non-inflationary stimulus with cut in government outlays equal to 1 per cent of GDP in the EEC (as per cent of base GDP)

Cut in income tax	1.47 to 1.83
Cut in household indirect taxes	0.86 or more
Cut in employers' social security contributions	0.98 or more

SOURCE: Derived from Dramais, 1986.
NOTE: as cuts in indirect taxes and in employers' social security contributions *reduce* prices as well as stimulating real output, there is (so far as this evidence goes, at any rate) no upper limit to the extent to which those taxes could be cut in the process of giving a non-inflationary stimulus. Indeed, there would be no need also to reduce government outlays in order to give a non-inflationary stimulus by cuts in either of those taxes, unless there was also some other aim, such as holding down the budget deficit or the deficit on the current account.

EFFECTS ON PRODUCTIVITY AND MONEY WAGE RATES

The results of the OECD simulations considered above also throw some light on the reasons why income tax cuts appear to have less upward effect on prices for a given effect on real output or employment.

One reason why the alternative forms of macroeconomic stimulus might have different effects on prices for a given effect on real output or employment could be if they had different effects on productivity – for it is clearly easier to hold down the price level if real output per head is rising relatively rapidly than if it is not.

Table 3.7 shows that the results of the OECD simulations imply that there may well be some (inverse) relationship between the ranking of the two *fiscal* forms of stimulus in terms of their effects on output per person employed ('productivity') on the one hand, and the extent to which they raise the price level (for a given real stimulus), on the other. For six of the countries (that is, excluding the US), it is income tax cuts that appear, on this evidence, to have the greater upward effect on productivity for a given stimulus to employment; for West Germany it is bond-financed income tax cuts, and for Japan, France, the UK, Italy and Canada a cut in income tax (with interest rates held constant) appears on these simulations to have the greater upward effect upon real GDP per person employed; and only for the US and Japan does a rise in government outlays (with interest rates fixed) have the greater upward effect on productivity per unit rise in real GNP/GDP. It may be of significance that for all these countries except the US and Germany a monetary stimulus has a greater upward effect on productivity than does any form of fiscal stimulus. It seems, therefore, on these figures, that the greater upward effect on prices exerted by monetary policy operates *despite* its greater upward effect on productivity.

These effects on productivity thus do little to explain the general superiority of income tax cuts over monetary expansion in terms of its comparative advantage in stimulating real output while minimising the upward pressure on prices; but for six of the countries these considerations appear to contribute towards explaining the superiority of income tax cuts over government outlays (from the same point of view). They do not, however, throw any light on the superiority of bond-financed income tax cuts over accommodated income tax cuts (except for the US and West Germany). For only two of the countries (West Germany and the US), however, this evidence suggests that these productivity considerations could help to explain why bond-financed government outlays score more highly than accommodated government outlays if a stimulus that minimises price increases is required.

Table 3.7 Effects of alternative forms of stimulus on real GNP/GDP for 1 percent rise in employment with floating exchange rates, seven major OECD countries (annual average over five years) (per cent)

	US	*Japan*	*West Germany*	*France*	*UK*	*Italy*	*Canada*
Income tax cut (money constant)	2.18	4.71	*2.33*	3.55	1.47	4.75	1.62
Income tax cut (interest rates constant)	1.82	5.07	1.30	3.62	1.61	6.00	1.71
Rise in government outlays (money constant)	*2.53*	1.99	2.06	2.65	1.17	5.22	1.42
Rise in government outlays (interest rates constant)	1.91	4.68	1.16	3.16	1.47	5.33	1.68
Cut in short-term interest rates	1.43	*5.12*	0.80	*5.33*	*1.77*	*	2.5

NOTE: the figure for the form of stimulus that has the greatest upward effect on productivity for each country is italicised.
* Signifies that the figure is undefined, as the measure does not increase employment, and therefore has the greatest upward effect on real GDP per person employed.
SOURCE: As for Table 3.1

Tables 3.8 and 3.9 show that for all seven countries a cut in short-term interest rates could be expected to cause a large depreciation in the process of stimulating real output or employment. By contrast, either of the fiscal measures with money held constant appears on this evidence to lead to an appreciation for five of the countries, but a depreciation (though a very much smaller one than does a cut in interest rates) for the US and Italy. (By the fifth year after the change it also caused a depreciation for Canada.) One might surmise that for Italy the existence of exchange controls over capital movements reduced the tendency for capital inflow to increase as interest rates rose in the face of a fiscal

Table 3.8 Effects of alternative forms of macroeconomic stimulus on the exchange rate for 1 per cent rise in real GNP/GDP, seven major OECD countries (annual average over five years, with effect in Year 5 in parentheses) (per cent)

	US	*Japan*	*West Germany*	*France*	*UK*	*Italy*	*Canada*
Cut in income tax, money constant	−0.62 (−2.00)	1.03 (1.50)	0.69 (0.50)	0.69 (0.91)	1.28 (1.50)	−0.16 (−0.57)	0.29 (−1.00)
Rise in government outlays, money constant	−1.09 (−4.25)	1.00 (0.00)	0.69 (0.40)	0.76 (1.00)	1.37 (1.67)	−0.32 (−1.17)	0.15 *
Cut in income tax, interest rates constant	−1.83 (−3.44)	−0.58 (1.22)	−0.74 (−1.18)	−0.21 (−0.75)	−1.78 (−3.90)	−0.74 (−1.75)	−1.61 (−3.11)
Rise in government outlays, interest rates constant	−2.37 (−4.86)	−0.73 (−1.56)	−0.86 (−1.75)	−0.72 (−1.19)	−2.34 (−5.09)	−1.02 (−2.50)	−2.02 (−4.50)
Cut in short term interest rates	−4.06 (−6.50)	−3.14 (−1.77)	−2.79 (−3.00)	−4.56 (−3.33)	−6.13 (−7.57)	−4.43 (−5.00)	−3.95 (−4.33)

NOTE: negative figures indicate *depreciation.*
* This figure is undefined, as for Canada by Year 5 this measure has no upward effect on real GDP.
SOURCE: as for Table 3.1.

stimulus (with money held constant), so that the dominant effect on the exchange rate was the weakening of the current account. For the US, in contrast to the other countries, the favourable effects on capital inflow resulting from upward pressure on interest rates resulting from either form of fiscal stimulus there would tend to be offset to a considerable extent by the tendency for interest rates in other countries to rise in sympathy. For the US also (though for very different reasons from those applicable to Italy) one would therefore expect the effects

Table 3.9 Effects of alternative forms of macroeconomic stimulus on the exchange rate for a 1 per cent rise in employment, seven major OECD countries (annual average over five years) (per cent)

	US	*Japan*	*West Germany*	*France*	*UK*	*Italy*	*Canada*
Cut in income tax (money constant)	−1.35	4.86	1.60	2.45	1.88	−0.75	0.46
Rise in government outlays (money constant)	−2.77	4.38	1.41	2.00	1.61	−1.44	0.21
Cut in income tax, interest rates constant	−3.34	−2.93	−0.95	−1.85	−2.86	−4.43	−2.76
Rise in government outlays, interest rates constant	−4.53	−3.21	−1.00	−2.26	−3.44	−5.44	−3.39
Cut in short-term interest rates	−5.83	−9.50	−2.23	−24.33	−10.85	*	−9.88

* For Italy a cut in interest rates gives no stimulus to employment, so that this figure is undefined. The extent of the depreciation for Italy resulting from the cut in short-term interest rates simulated is, however, greater than for any of the other seven countries except France.
SOURCE: as for Table 3.1.

on capital inflow of the upward pressure on interest rates with a fiscal expansion (again, without monetary accommodation) to be less than for the other six countries (by comparison with its effects through the current account). It is not surprising that by the fifth year after the change this was true for Canada also, in view of its close links with the US capital market.

Of the two stimulatory fiscal measures with money held constant, income tax cuts had the greater tendency to cause appreciation (or, for the US and Italy – and by year 5 also for Canada – less tendency to cause depreciation) for five of the seven countries. For France and the

UK, however, both for the average of the five years and in year 5, government outlays had the greater effect in the direction of strengthening the exchange rate for a given stimulus to real *output*; though even for those two countries income tax cuts tended to cause more appreciation than did a rise in government outlays for a given stimulus to *employment*.

These tables also show that if the two forms of fiscal stimulus were accompanied by monetary measures to hold down interest rates, the extent of the depreciation was in all cases greater (or the extent of any appreciation, less) than with money held constant – as one would expect; for the lower level of interest rates under the accommodated forms of stimulus naturally meant that there is not in this case the incentive of higher interest rates to encourage additional capital inflow. Moreover, it may also be seen that, for each of the seven countries, an accommodated cut in income tax also led to less depreciation than did an accommodated rise in government spending.

Generally speaking, therefore, these effects operating through the exchange rate contribute considerably to explaining the superiority of fiscal measures over monetary measures in providing a real stimulus with minimal upward effect on prices (so far as that depends on effects operating through the exchange rate). These exchange rate considerations also contribute to explaining the superiority from this point of view of income tax cuts over increases in government outlays; and for all of the countries, and for both fiscal instruments, these exchange rate considerations appear to contribute to explaining why the accommodated forms of fiscal expansion had greater upward effect on prices (for a given real stimulus) than the bond-financed alternative.

As Table 3.10 shows, however, the effects operating through the exchange rate were certainly not the sole channels through which monetary policy was, for most countries, more inflationary than either form of fiscal stimulus. For the OECD has provided also simulations of the apparent effects of the alternative measures holding exchange rates constant; and this enables us to assess the relative importance of the exchange rate channel compared with other channels through which the different measures operated.

These simulations show that increases in government outlays would for five of the seven countries be the form of stimulus most likely to increase prices if the exchange rate were held constant; in other words, the channel through which monetary expansion tended to be the most inflationary form of stimulus under floating exchange rates was through its effect on the exchange rate itself. But it may also be seen from Table 3.10 that in only three of those five countries (Japan, West

Table 3.10 Effects on prices of alternative forms of stimulus for 1 per cent rise in real GNP/GDP, with fixed exchange rates, seven major OECD countries (annual average over five years) (per cent)

	US	*Japan*	*West Germany*	*France*	*UK*	*Italy*	*Canada*
Rise in government outlays, money constant	*2.32*	*0.98*	*0.84*	*0.51*	1.16	0.44	*2.92*
Income tax cut money constant	1.81	0.84	0.72	0.34	0.75	*1.71*	1.90
Rise in government outlays interest rates money constant	2.12	0.61	0.67	0.48	1.59	0.43	1.69
Income tax cut interest rates constant	1.67	0.54	0.60	0.35	1.23	0.31	1.02
Cut in short-term interest rates	1.96	0.39	0.30	0.36	*1.87*	0.60	*

* For this measure, there is no upward effect on prices for Canada, so that the figure is undefined, and the policy measure the least inflationary.
For each country the figure italicised is the *most* inflationary.
SOURCE: Derived from Richardson, 1987 and 1988 and data supplied by him.

Germany and Canada) was monetary policy less inflationary than either of the fiscal measures if the exchange rate were held constant. Moreover, of the two fiscal measures, government outlays remained more inflationary than income tax cuts (for a given effect on either real output or employment) even if the exchange rate were held constant provided either that both were bond-financed or both were accommodated by holding interest rates constant.

One should conclude, therefore, on this evidence, that for all the countries except Japan, Germany and Canada purely internal channels were of some significance in contributing to the greater upward effect on prices of monetary forms of stimulus with floating exchange rates, even though the effects operating through the exchange rate were probably the dominant channel for most or all of these countries.

Even abstracting from exchange rate effects (by using the simulations with the exchange rate held constant), however, income tax cuts were usually less inflationary than government outlays but not monetary expansion; so that the internal channels were presumably the dominant ones in explaining the comparative advantage of income tax cuts over government outlays or monetary expansion in stimulating output with least upward effect on prices. This also suggests that if one is comparing the relative effects on prices and on real output of alternative measures so far as they operate within countries (rather than through the exchange rate) there is not a clear dichotomy between government outlays and tax cuts on the one hand and monetary policy on the other – an especially clear illustration of the principle that the dichotomy of 'monetary versus fiscal' policy can be seriously misleading.

EFFECTS ON MONEY WAGE RATES OR EARNINGS

As Tables 3.11 and 3.12 show, for each of the seven countries, money wage rates rose by more, for any given rise in real GDP or employment, when the fiscal stimulus took the form of a rise in government expenditure than when it consisted of a cut in income tax rates. This clearly suggests that in all seven countries the effect of income tax cuts was to give less stimulus to money wage increases than did a rise in government outlays having the same effect on real GDP or employment.

For all the countries except the US, Canada and Japan wage rates rose more (for a given stimulus to real output or employment) when the stimulus took the form of a cut in short-term interest rates than with either of the two fiscal stimuli. For the US, a rise in government outlays had the biggest apparent upward effect on money wage rates and the effect of a cut in interest rates was intermediate in this respect between the two fiscal stimuli, while for Canada the monetary expansion has less upward effect on money wage rates than did either fiscal stimulus (Table 3.11). This helps to identify (if not to explain) the difference between the two North American countries (on the one hand) and the remaining countries (on the other) in terms of the relative effects on prices of the different measures tested.

As Table 3.13 shows, the apparent effect on nominal earnings in the UK of a cut in VAT or in employers' national insurance contributions was downwards in three models, and that of a cut in income tax was

Table 3.11 Effect on money wage rates of alternative measures for 1 per cent rise in real GNP/GDP with floating exchange rates, seven major OECD countries (change in average level over five years compared with base) (per cent)

	US	*Japan*	*West Germany*	*France*	*UK*	*Italy*	*Canada*
Income tax cut (money constant)	2.11	1.09	0.43	0.28	0.60	0.84	2.33
Income tax cut (interest rates constant)	2.17	1.08	0.88	0.55	1.69	1.05	1.86
Rise in government outlays (money constant)	3.03	1.26	0.54	0.40	0.96	1.15	3.22
Rise in government outlays (interest rates constant)	2.77	1.19	1.00	0.70	2.21	1.40	2.23
Cut in short-term interest rates	2.94	1.22	1.39	1.81	3.48	3.33	1.30

SOURCE: as for Table 3.1.

downwards in two of the models. The models give widely differing results about the ranking of the other measures in terms of their effects on nominal earnings.

COMPARISON WITH AN ALTERNATIVE APPROACH

The above results from simulations with large macroeconomic models may be compared with one adopting a very different standpoint to assessing the ranking of the principal macroeconomic instruments, but which also provides evidence that monetary policy is the most inflationary for any real stimulus that it might provide, and that tax cuts are the

Table 3.12 Effects on money wage rates for 1 per cent rise in employment, with floating exchange rates, seven major OECD countries (change in average level over five years as per cent of base) (per cent)

	US	*Japan*	*West Germany*	*France*	*UK*	*Italy*	*Canada*
Income tax cut (money constant)	4.59	5.14	1.00	1.00	0.88	4.00	3.76
Income tax cut (interest rates constant)	3.97	5.47	1.14	2.00	2.71	6.29	3.19
Rise in government outlays (money constant)	7.69	5.50	1.12	1.06	1.13	5.22	4.58
Rise on government outlays (interest rates constant)	5.29	5.58	1.16	2.21	3.25	7.44	3.74
Cut in short-term interest rates	4.22	6.25	1.11	9.67	6.15	*	3.25

* For Italy this measure has no upward effect on employment – so that, given the upward effect on prices, this figure would be undefined.
SOURCE: as for Table 3.1.

least inflationary (and likely to provide the most reliable stimulus), with government outlays being intermediate in these respects between the other two.[3]

This other approach assessed whether there was a statistically significant relationship between changes in the three main macroeconomic instruments, as measured in this case by changes in the (cylically adjusted) level of government outlays and taxes, together with monetary growth rates, and changes in the consumer price index in a country and also with its level of unemployment over the three succeeding years,

Table 3.13 Effect of alternative forms of stimulus on average nominal earnings for 1 per cent rise real GDP in the UK (effect on average level over five years as per cent of base) (per cent)

Model / *Stimulus*	*LBS*	*NIESR*	*HMT*	*B of E*	*Average of the four models*
Cut in VAT*	1.74	−0.55	−1.69	−3.56	−1.01
Cut in employers' national insurance contributions*	11.82	−0.87	−0.93	−0.74	2.32
Cut in income tax*	2.86	1.62	−0.28	−3.11	0.27
Rise in government outlays*	1.63	1.29	2.54	0.96	1.61
Rise in government outlays (money constant)	0.69	1.14	10.75	0.93	3.38
Cut in short-term interest rates	2.52	1.52	1.34	2.99	4.45

* With interest rates held constant.
SOURCE: Derived from Fisher *et al.*, 1988.

pooling the year-to-year data for 15 OECD countries for the years 1967 to 1984.

This study found that monetary policy (as thus measured) has a statistically significant (positive) relationship with the rise in prices over the immediately ensuing years, but not with unemployment rates; that, at the other extreme, tax cuts tended to be associated with falling unemployment in the following years, but not to have any clear relationship (positive or negative) with price changes in those years (which would be consistent with the above evidence that some types of tax cuts tend to increase prices and others to reduce them); while government outlays did not have a statistically significant apparent effect on unemployment, and (on one formulation) tended to be followed by higher rates of inflation or (on another formulation) not to have a significant relationship with prices in either direction.

In other words, monetary policy was more inflationary than either fiscal stimulus for any given real effect it might have; tax cuts had an apparently significant effect in reducing unemployment (but not in affecting prices); while government outlays were intermediate between the other two in that they had no apparently significant effect on unemployment and a less significant effect than monetary policy upon prices.

CONCLUSIONS

The following are the conclusions about policies that could provide a non-inflationary stimulus that can be drawn from the evidence considered in this chapter.

(1) A cut in value-added taxation, or indirect taxes generally, is either a measure likely to reduce prices while raising output and employment (even when taken alone), or else (according to one model) it can be combined with certain other tax increases or a tightening of monetary policy to achieve both a fall in prices and a rise in output or employment. None of the evidence is inconsistent with this prescription.

(2) A bond-financed cut in income tax exerts less upward pressure on prices than a bond-financed rise in government outlays, for a given stimulus to both real output and employment. Some combinations of income-tax cuts and reductions in government outlays are therefore likely to be available that will both reduce prices and raise output or employment. Again, none of this evidence is inconsistent with this prescription.

(3) A cut in employers' national insurance contributions or social security contributions is also likely (on all these pieces of evidence except one) to be an instrument that will both reduce prices and stimulate output and employment. The evidence of one model implies that for the UK a cut in national insurance contributions could not be combined with any other measure in such a way as to reduce prices while raising real *output*; but even on the evidence from that model a cut in employers' national insurance contributions could still be combined with either a rise in income taxation (even with the rate of interest held constant) or a rise in interest rates in such a way as to reduce prices and raise *employment*.

(4) A bond-financed cut in income tax is less inflationary than a cut in interest rates for a given effect on *employment* for all countries; so that a cut in income tax coupled with a tightening of monetary policy in an appropriate combination could both raise *employment* and reduce the upward pressure on prices in all countries for which these measures have both been simulated. But for Canada that combination of measures could not be used to stimulate real *output* while reducing

prices, if one accepts the OECD evidence that for Canada a cut in short-term interest rates is *less* inflationary than a bond-financed cut in income tax (or a bond-financed rise in government outlays) for a given effect on real *output*. The appropriate combination for Canada to give a non-inflationary stimulus would thus (on this evidence) be to *ease* monetary policy and *tighten* one of the fiscal instruments; or, alternatively, as for the other countries, to cut income tax and reduce government outlays in appropriate combinations.

(5) The evidence would suggest, on balance, that it is probably also true that a cut in short-term interest rates is more inflationary than a rise in government outlays or income tax cuts (though this is less likely to be true if the fiscal measures are accommodated rather than being bond-financed). It also appears to be likely that fiscal measures of expansion are less inflationary for a given real stimulus if they are bond-financed than if they are accommodated by monetary policy directed at holding down interest rates. But Canada, and perhaps the US, may be exceptions to these two conclusions, at least in part. Outside North America, however, some combination of tight monetary policy with fiscal stimulus – especially if the fiscal stimulus is bond financed, and if it takes the form of a tax cut – is likely to be available that will both stimulate real output and employment and also tend to reduce prices. For the US and Canada the appropriate combinations are most likely to be either cuts in income tax coupled with reductions in government outlays, or, alternatively, an *easing* of monetary policy with some form of fiscal restraint, preferably economies in government outlays.

NOTES

1. See Wallis *et al*, 1987 and Fisher *et al*, 1988 (the results of the latter being used here).
2. See Dramais, 1986.
3. See Perkins and Tran Van Hoa, 1987 and Appendix to Perkins, 1985.

4 Dealing with Two Macroeconomic Problems

The *a priori* arguments in Chapter 2 and the empirical evidence in Chapter 3 imply that there are various combinations of macroeconomic policy instruments that can be used to work towards the achievement of higher real output or employment, so long as there are spare resources in the economy, without increasing prices, and even while reducing the upward pressure on prices. In the present chapter we shall consider a framework of analysis to deal with the choice of appropriate combinations of policy measures to achieve these aims.

Any two macroeconomic instruments could have been chosen by way of illustration: but in the following examples we shall take the two instruments to be a rise in the general level of government outlays (for which an easing of monetary policy could be substituted) and a cut in the general level of taxes.

We consider the following cases.

(i) There may be an instrument that has a negligible effect on output but a large upward effect on prices, whereas another instrument has a considerable upward effect on both objectives.

For example, assume that the relative effects of these two instruments are as shown in Table 4.1. (The units in which the effects of the instruments in this and other tables in this chapter are expressed are essentially arbitrary, as it is the *ratio* of the effects of each instrument on one of the objectives *for a given effect on the other* that is relevant

Table 4.1 Two fiscal instruments, one having no effect on output

	Tax cuts	*Government outlays*
Effect on		
Output	+1	0
Prices	+1	1

Table 4.2 Two fiscal instruments with different relative effects on two objectives

	Tax cuts	*Government outlays*
Effect on		
Output	+1	+1
Prices	+1	+2

to the policy decisions. But the units may be thought of as percentage changes in each of the objectives over some stated period.)

In this case it is obvious that if one wants to exert downward pressure on prices while raising output, government outlays should be reduced and taxes cut to an appropriate extent until the two objectives are achieved; for in this case a cut in government outlays would not have any (unwanted) downward effect on output.

(ii) Even if each instrument has some effect on both objectives, the desired result can be achieved by appropriate adjustments of both of them, provided only that their respective (upward) effects on prices are not the same for a given upward effect on output.

For example, assume that their relative effects are as shown Table 4.2. Then, if taxes are cut sufficiently to raise output by one unit, the consequent upward effect on prices can be offset by a reduction in government outlays of an amount that would reduce output by only 0.5 of a unit; so that, taking the effects of both measures together, there would be a net stimulus to real output without a net rise in prices. A slightly greater reduction in government outlays would thus make it possible to reduce prices while raising real output. An example of a change that would (on the same assumptions) have this effect would be as in Table 4.3.

Table 4.3 Combinations of two instruments to raise output and reduce prices

	Tax cuts	*Reduction in government outlays*	*Net effect*
Effect on			
Output	+1	−0.6	+0.4
Prices	+1	−1.2	−0.2

Indeed, any cut in government outlays sufficient to reduce output by more than 0.5 of a unit but less than one unit can be combined with a tax cut that raises output by one unit, to give both a net rise in output and downward pressure on prices.

It should be observed that if the government were unwise enough to try to *raise* tax rates with the aim of checking inflation, while also increasing government outlays, with the intention of thereby reducing unemployment) for any given rate of increase in prices, or both reduce at any given level of real output, or reduce output (increase unemployment) for any given rate of increase in prices, or both reduce real output (make unemployment worse) and increase the upward pressure on prices.

For example, if it raised tax rates by enough to reduce prices by one unit, and then tried to offset the consequent reduction in real output by increasing government outlays, the consequent net increase in the price level at any given level of real output (or fall in real output for any given net upward effect on prices) would clearly lead to a situation that would be inferior to that which would result from tax cuts and an appropriate reduction in government outlays (assuming of course that the aim was to give a non-inflationary, or even price-reducing, stimulus).

Table 4.4 illustrates this, on the same assumptions as in those used for the previous example.

It is thus clear that if a government determines what changes to make in its *outlays* with the aim of affecting *real output*, and what changes

Table 4.4 Two fiscal instruments with an inappropriate assignment to objectives

	Rise in *taxes*	***Cut in*** *government outlays*	*Net effect*
Effect on			
Output	−1	+1	0
Prices	−1	+2	+1
or			
Effect on			
Output	−1	+1.2	+0.2
Prices	−1	+2.4	+1.4
or			
Effect on			
Output	−1	+0.8	−0.2
Prices	−1	+1.6	+0.6

to make in its *tax rates* with the aim of *reducing inflation*, it will (on these assumptions) bring about some inferior combination of macroeconomic outcomes, compared with the opposite policy of directing tax changes towards the aim of stimulating real output, and government outlays towards that of exerting downward pressure on prices (assuming that its aim is to raise output and to hold down inflation, or to work towards one of those objectives without moving the economy away from the other).[1]

It is true that if the government knew exactly what combination of changes in the instruments would most quickly and efficiently move the economy towards the desired macroeconomic situation, it should set the instruments at the appropriate levels. As no government has such an exact knowledge of the relevant figures, however, policy makers are normally accustomed to think of themselves as 'assigning' an instrument to an objective: that is, to changing the setting of it primarily with an eye to its effect on a particular objective. Provided that the government has a reasonably good idea about which of the available instruments will have the most helpful effect on each of its objectives with the minimum of adverse effect (or, of course, ideally, with a helpful effect) on the achievement of its other macroeconomic objective, it can change the setting of each of the instruments in directions that can be expected to improve the general macroeconomic situation. But if it changes the setting of each instrument with an eye to affecting the objective for which that instrument is relatively *less* well suited, the result is bound to be a less favourable macroeconomic situation than could otherwise have been achieved. It is therefore important that policy makers should know as much as possible about the relative effect of each of the available instruments on each of the objectives in which they are interested, and then decide the changes to be made in each of these instruments in the light of the information they have about these relative effects.

'TWO-BIRD' INSTRUMENTS

(iii) There may be an instrument that can be changed in such a way as to increase real output (or employment) while exerting downward pressure on prices.

If it is true that some forms of tax cut actually reduce prices as well as stimulating output (as much of the evidence discussed in Chapter 3 suggests may be true of certain types of tax cut), then it is clearly possible to 'kill two birds with one stone', as a cut in the taxes in question would bring the state of the economy closer to both of the macro objectives, without the need to make any adjustment in other instruments, such as government outlays or monetary policy. We shall therefore term any such policy instruments 'two-bird' instruments.[2]

In the same way, if some forms of tax cut reduce prices and others raise them, an appropriate shift between the two types of tax – reducing those taxes that tend to raise prices and increasing those taxes that tend to reduce prices – can presumably be used to exert downward pressure on prices without necessarily reducing tax revenue, and even to give a stimulus to real output at the same time. This carries the implication that such a shift in the relative importance of these two different types of tax (with total tax revenue being kept unchanged) may have two distinct upward effects on prices. For if a rise in indirect taxes tends to raise prices, whereas a rise in income tax rates tends to reduce prices (as is suggested by almost all the evidence in Chapter 3), this means that a shift from direct to indirect taxes will tend to raise the price level on two counts: for the rise in indirect taxes will increase prices, as will also the reduction in direct taxes.

If there are any two-bird instruments, it is obviously very important to know of their existence: for if any such instrument is moved in the *wrong* direction it can clearly both increase prices and reduce real output.

If there are no such instruments available, or if a greater downward effect on prices is required for a given real stimulus than would result from a cut in indirect tax rates sufficient to provide that stimulus, appropriate combinations of two or more instruments will be required. Even confining attention to three broad instruments – monetary policy, government outlays, and the general level of taxation – there are likely to be many combinations of two (or all) of these instruments that can raise output without increasing the upward effect on prices, even if every individual instrument taken alone would tend to make inflation worse in the process of stimulating real output and employment. The general prescription is clearly to move the *less* inflationary of any two instruments in the *expansionary* direction, while offsetting the consequent upward effect on prices by moving the *more* inflationary instrument to an appropriate extent in a *contractionary* direction.

With three instruments, each of which has a different effect on prices for a given real stimulus, a government clearly has a choice of combinations of changes to choose from. If monetary policy is the most inflationary, tax cuts the least inflationary, and government outlays intermediate between the other two in their upward effects on prices (for a given real stimulus) – the ranking implied by most of the empirical evidence in Chapter 3 – a government wishing to provide a non-inflationary (or price-reducing) stimulus can do so (i) by tightening monetary policy and cutting tax rates; or (ii) by cutting both government outlays and tax rates; or (iii) by tightening monetary policy and increasing government outlays (to an appropriate extent in each case).

(iv) Each instrument may affect a different objective, and only that objective.

An extreme example of the foregoing case would be if there are two instruments each of which affects a different objective, and *only* that objective. The possibility of such cases cannot be ruled out. For we have seen in Chapter 3 that some types of tax cut tend to raise prices and others to reduce them, so that there must be combinations of different types of tax cut (perhaps something close to a flat across-the-board cut in all types of tax simultaneously) that would have a negligible net effect on prices in the process of providing a real stimulus. There is also some evidence (also in Chapter 3) that suggests that, after an initial stimulus, an expansionary monetary policy may have little or no effect in raising employment in some countries – so that its only effect in those cases will thus eventually be on prices. If so, each of those two instruments can and must obviously be varied with an eye merely to affecting the objective that it is able to influence.

The case where each instrument can affect only one objective – each of them a different objective – is not worth illustrating by an example; for, clearly, each instrument must then be changed in the direction that will have the desired effect on the only objective that it can influence; and that change will not, in that case, have any undesired side-effects on the other objective.

THE WRONG ASSIGNMENT OF INSTRUMENTS

One implication of the foregoing discussion is that if instruments are changed mainly, or even partly, with an eye to influencing the macroeconomic objective for which they are least (less) suited, the economy will be driven away from one or more of its macroeconomic objectives. Even if all the available instruments are varied simultaneously with an eye to working towards the same objective – for example, to reducing inflation – if taxes are increased considerably and monetary policy is simultaneously tightened, the combination of effects that is to be expected will be a downward impact on employment and on real output greater than if each of those instruments had been varied with an eye to the macroeconomic objective on which it had the greater relative effect. A worse combination of output and inflation would then result than if the principal reliance had been placed on a tight monetary policy to exert downward pressure on prices – without the tax increases, and preferably together with tax cuts. (A concentration of all, or several, instruments mainly, or wholly, on the aim of 'stopping inflation first' was probably responsible for much of the stagflation of the later 1970s and early 1980s.)

THE FISCAL BALANCE AND ALTERNATIVE FORMS OF STIMULUS

One consideration that may inhibit governments from adopting price-reducing forms of expansionary action, or combinations of measures that would raise output as much as possible with little or no upward pressure on prices, may be fears about the likely effects of such a stimulus upon the fiscal balance (the 'budget deficit', or 'public sector borrowing requirement'). This approach almost implies that the government is considering the fiscal balance as an objective in its own right. Without accepting the view that this *ought* to be a relevant consideration in the choice of instruments to maximise the helpful macroeconomic effects, in view of the weight that governments often attach to such considerations it is appropriate to consider the relative effects of alternative instruments, especially of alternative fiscal instruments, on the fiscal balance, to see whether those effects are likely to constitute any serious political obstacle to choosing a mix of instruments that will further both main macroeconomic objectives.

The first point to observe is that measures of monetary expansion are likely to reduce the fiscal deficit (or increase the fiscal surplus), as they do *not* operate through increases in the outlay side or reductions in the revenue side of the budget, and their upward effect on nominal income will tend to increase revenue. By contrast, any of the available forms of fiscal stimulus will, taken by itself, normally tend to move the fiscal balance in the direction of deficit (at any given level of employment or real output – the 'cyclically adjusted' or 'structural' fiscal balance). Unfortunately, as we have seen in Chapters 2 and 3, monetary expansion tends to be the least effective stimulus for raising real output or employment without considerable upward pressure on prices, and combinations of fiscal changes are far more likely to be able to do this. Moreover, the combination of monetary contraction with one of the forms of fiscal stimulus is likely to worsen the fiscal balance.

But the OECD evidence (on which Table 4.5 is based) for the seven major countries suggests that a rise in government spending will, for all countries except Canada and (marginally) Japan, have a greater upward effect on the fiscal deficit than will a cut in income tax rates having the same effect on *real output*.

Moreover, the tests for the EEC as a whole, while confirming the conclusions that may be drawn from the OECD simulations about the relative effects of government outlays and income tax cuts upon the fiscal balance (for a given real stimulus) also compare the effects of different forms of tax cut, and these comparisons imply that other forms of tax cut – cuts in household indirect taxes and reductions in employers' social security contributions – have a much smaller upward effect on the budget deficit (or a smaller downward effect on the budget surplus) than do income tax cuts for a given real stimulus (see Table 4.6).

Putting these two pieces of evidence together, therefore, it seems likely that a cut in the general level of taxes across the board would have a smaller upward effect on any budget deficit (or downward effect on any budget surplus) than would a rise in the general level of government outlays for a given upward effect on real output – at least for the

Table 4.5 Effects on fiscal balance of alternative fiscal measures for 1 per cent stimulus to real GDP, seven major OECD countries (annual average over five years) (per cent of base GNP/GDP)

	US	*Japan*	*West Germany*	*France*	*UK*	*Italy*	*Canada*
Rise in government outlays (money constant)	−1.73	−1.71	−1.46	−2.09	−2.63	−2.59	−3.22
Income tax cut (money constant)	−1.46	−1.73	−1.43	−1.87	−2.56	−2.11	−3.48

SOURCE: as for Table 3.1.

Table 4.6 Effects on fiscal balance of change in various fiscal measures to give 1 per cent stimulus to real GDP, EEC (annual average over five years) (per cent of base GDP)

Rise in government outlays	−0.80
Cut in household direct taxes	−1.23
Cut in household indirect taxes	−0.63
Cut in employers' social security contributions	−0.55

SOURCE: Derived from Dramais, 1986.

countries covered by these simulations, and judging on the basis of this evidence.

It is true that one should not expect that the exact quantitative effect on the fiscal balance of any two or more of these measures taken simultaneously would be the same as the sum of the likely effects of each of them taken separately. But there is no reason to suppose that the *direction* of the net effect on the fiscal balance of reducing government outlays and simultaneously reducing across the board all the taxes for which the simulations are shown in Table 4.6 would be different from that suggested by the addition of their separately simulated effects. There is also a presumption from this evidence that a cut in both government outlays and income tax on a scale that would hold real GDP constant for most of the major OECD countries would be to increase the fiscal surplus (as suggested by the separate results for each of these measures shown in Table 4.5). Taken together with the evidence about the relative effects on prices, for a given stimulus to real GDP, of government outlays on the one hand and income tax cuts on the other, there thus appear likely for most major countries to be changes in the composition of the budget that can reduce a budget deficit (or increase any fiscal surplus) while providing a non-inflationary real stimulus.

This means that, if the aim is to avoid moving the budget in the direction of deficit, as much as possible of any desired stimulus should be given by way of cuts in indirect taxes or of taxes on labour inputs, and as little as possible by way of general rises in government outlays. It may also be better (if the government wishes to minimise the tendency for the budget deficit to rise) to give a stimulus by way of income tax cuts rather than by rises in government outlays, though the evidence on this is mixed, and this may be true for some countries but not others.

Moreover, to judge from the simulations for the EEC, those combinations of fiscal measures that are most likely to provide a non-inflationary (or price-reducing) stimulus are generally also those that are likely to constitute the forms of fiscal stimulus that will have the least adverse, or most favourable, effect on the fiscal balance – so that fears about these effects on the fiscal balance ought not, on the above evidence, to inhibit governments from adopting appropriate combinations of fiscal measures for exerting downward pressure on prices while increasing real output.

The most general conclusion from the above argument is that the provision of a fiscal stimulus should not be identified with a movement of the budget in the direction of deficit (at any given level of real output or employment). For there are combinations of measures that will provide a real stimulus and which will also reduce the fiscal deficit, as well as others that will increase it or leave it unchanged. Certainly, if a government is inhibited from adopting expansionary fiscal measures by fears about the effect on the fiscal balance, those fears appear, at least on the evidence cited above, to be, in general, misguided.

BALANCED BUDGET INCREASES

The evidence from the OECD simulations summarised in Table 4.5 also implies that a balanced budget increase – even in the form of an equal rise in government outlays and in income tax (the form of tax change simulated in the OECD tests) – may well have a contractionary effect upon real GDP, even though it also appears likely to have an *upward* effect on *nominal* GDP. There is only one case among the countries tested where a net stimulus to real GDP appears likely, on this evidence, to result from a rise in income tax receipts equal to a rise in government outlays. This is Japan, where the ratio of both taxes and government outlays to GDP was lower than in the other countries covered, and where the price and cost-increasing effects of raising both sides of the budget may therefore have been less than in the other countries (for a given nominal stimulus). There is also one case where a balanced budget expansion in this form has a downward effect even on *nominal* GDP. It is thus clearly important to take account not only of the effect of fiscal changes on nominal aggregate demand, but also of the decomposition of any resulting change in aggregate demand between real output (or employment), on the one hand, and prices, on the other. For otherwise there is a very real danger that governments who are counting on a balanced budget increase to raise aggregate demand will find themselves adopting combinations of fiscal measures that lead to a contraction of real output and employment. The EEC evidence implies that there is a much greater risk of a balanced budget increase proving to be contractionary in real terms if the taxes that are increased are household indirect taxes or employers' social security contributions than if they are household income taxes.

In any case, an equal rise in both sides of the budget should not be described as a 'balanced budget *expansion*', for that phrase begs the vitally important question of whether a balanced budget *increase* is, or is not, in fact 'expansionary' in terms of its effect on real output or employment.

CONCLUSION

If the only concerns of a government are to raise real output and to reduce the upward pressure on prices, it is possible for it to do so provided that there are at least two macroeconomic instruments that raise prices to different degrees for a given stimulus to real output. This will involve changing the setting of one of these instruments (the less inflationary of the two) in an expansionary direction and the other (the more inflationary) in a contractionary direction if a non-inflationary or price-reducing stimulus is required.

It also means that if all the available macroeconomic instruments tend to raise prices in the process of giving a stimulus to real output it will be possible to prevent a real stimulus from increasing prices *only* if one of the more inflationary of the two instruments is moved in a contractionary dirrection to an appropriate extent when a stimulus is being given by means of the other. If all the macroeconomic instruments are of this nature, therefore – tending to raise prices when they give a real stimulus – if the aim is to provide a non-inflationary stimulus it will thus be important always to move one of the more inflationary instruments in a contractionary direction when a stimulus is being given by one of the less inflationary ones.

Perhaps the main reason why it has come to be generally believed that any policy that gives a real stimulus is bound to be inflationary is that governments would normally consider it odd, or even self-contradictory, to tighten one policy measure while easing another. This is probably an important reason why the world as a whole has generally experienced an unwelcome combination of price rises and loss of potential output over most of the period since the late 1960s (and, incidentally, also why so-called 'Keynesian' fiscal policies to reduce unemployment have in some quarters earned a bad name over those years). The primary reason for this is presumably that macroeconomic policy formulation and discussion has not usually been in terms of the relative effects of the different instruments on the different objectives; and has not therefore led to the varying of the combinations of these instruments in such a way as to work as efficiently as possible towards both of the major macroeconomic objectives simultaneously.

At the same time, if, as appears to be likely, there are also instruments that operate in the desired direction on *both* objectives – tending to exert *downward* pressure on prices while stimulating real output – it is clearly of crucial importance to move any such instruments in the direction that will further both these aims of policy. For, clearly, if a government increases taxes of types that both raise prices and reduce output (in the misguided hope that this will help to reduce inflation), such a policy will obviously make both macroeconomic problems worse. Again, it seems likely that failure to identify such instruments – or perhaps the widespread assumption that they do not exist – has led governments to try to check inflation partly by raising taxes of this type, and thus tending to reduce output below its potential, as well as increasing the upward pressure on prices at any given level of real output or employment. Evidence cited in the preceding chapter suggests that a wide range of indirect taxes and taxes on employers related to the number of people they employ (employers' national insurance contributions in the UK and employers' social security contributions in the EEC) are of this nature. If that is true, then the quickest way of raising output and reducing the upward pressure on prices would be to reduce such taxes. If the aim was to do this without a loss of revenue it would be appropriate to replace such taxes by other types of tax (mainly income taxes) that do not tend to raise prices in the process of restraining output, provided that those other taxes do not have as great a downward effect (per unit of revenue collected) on real output or employment as do the price-increasing forms of taxation.

The evidence cited above also suggests that the combinations of fiscal measures that are most likely to provide a non-inflationary stimulus are generally those least likely to increase the fiscal deficit. At the very least, it is indefensible to assume that a rise in the fiscal deficit is *required* in order to provide a real stimulus – still less to *identify* the provision of such a stimulus with an increase in the (cyclically adjusted) fiscal deficit.

NOTES

1. The present writer has argued elsewhere that it was a tendency for governments to raise both government outlays and taxes as a proportion of total output – as well as to adopt generally lax monetary policies – that was largely responsible for the upward pressure on both prices and unemployment in most OECD countries between the late 1960s and the early 1980s. (See Perkins, 1985.) The greater macroeconomic success of the middle and later 1980s may be partly attributable to the tendency for many countries to slow down or even arrest the rise in both government outlays and taxes in relation to total output during that decade, as well as to adopt tighter monetary measures. But the failure to reduce taxes as a proportion of total output in many countries (or at least the failure to do this on a sufficient scale) may be the reason why, even in those years, macroeconomic policies were less successful in holding down unemployment and inflation than in some earlier decades.
2. In one sense, *any* instrument might in some circumstances be a 'two-bird instrument'. For instance, it might conceivably happen that a government wished to increase output while exerting *upward* pressure on prices – in which case it could make use of a number of different individual instruments. The definition of a 'two-bird' instrument used above is from the standpoint that the relevant cases in the real contemporary world are likely to be where a government wishes to give a non-inflationary (or price-reducing) stimulus. But in the most general framework of analysis one should bear in mind that the government of some country, at some time, might happen to wish to move the economy in both (or all of) the directions that will result from a given change in *any* single instrument.

5 The Macroeconomic Mix in the Open Economy: Basic Arguments

When we proceed to consider not only those macroeconomic objectives that relate to the internal aspects of the economy but also those that relate to the 'open' or international aspects of an economy, we have to adopt a framework for thinking about macroeconomic policy that embraces three, rather than only two, objectives. We are still interested in holding down unemployment and inflation, but we must now add an objective that relates to the state of a country's balance of payments on current account, usually considered in the context of its international debtor/creditor position (which is the outcome of the current account surpluses or deficits that it has run in past). The reason for including the cumulative creditor or debtor position of the country as one aspect of the external balance objective is that a country that has large net external assets is clearly much less likely to feel under pressure to reduce a current account deficit of a given order than one with heavy external indebtedness.

We shall not here be considering whether or not a government is right to consider such objectives, but merely take it that governments do in fact take them into account in formulating their macroeconomic policy. The discussion focuses on asking how the external objectives that governments take into account may best be achieved along with the objectives of high growth (or low unemployment) and low inflation discussed in earlier chapters. (There is in fact a good case for the view that governments ought to leave it to the market to determine how much the private sector borrows overseas, and to that extent the state of the current account balance; and that the government's own overseas borrowing or lending should also be determined on the basis of the social costs and benefits of the loans; so that macroeconomic policy as such should not in fact take the state of the current account balance as one of its objectives.)

If excessive current account deficits (or surpluses) were always associated with domestic excess (or inadequate) demand, so that the only influence upon the state of a country's current account was the matter of whether it was operating at full employment (or below or above that level), the current account would not in fact be worth considering as an additional objective. But a country may have a very large current account surplus (and a strong international creditor position), yet be unable or unwilling to take corrective action, at least by way of expansionary macroeconomic measures, for fear that this may lead to inflation. Or a country with an excessive current account deficit may be satisfied with its level of activity and rate of inflation, and consequently be reluctant to take action – at least of a contractionary nature – to try to reduce a current account deficit, for fear of upsetting its state of internal balance. In such cases, it is clearly of importance to a country to know whether there are combinations of macroeconomic instruments available that will enable it to move closer to the desired state of its current account without prejudicing the achievement of its internal macroeconomic objectives.

A country is likely to require at least three instruments of macroeconomic policy in order to try to keep the economy as close as possible to the desired macroeconomic objectives. This will generally involve having at least three instruments with different relative effects on each of the three objectives. In order to use these instruments appropriately, therefore, we need to know the main considerations that determine their relative effects on the three objectives, except in cases where it may happen that the use of a single instrument by itself is able to move the economy in the desired direction in terms of two (or even all) of the macroeconomic objectives.

In addition to discussing the likely effects of various macroeconomic instruments upon the state of the country's net current account balance, we shall also take account of a broader objective, of which the state of the current account is only part. This is the net change in a country's total (internal and external) wealth over the period of interest to the policy maker. This comprises the net addition to the country's stock of useful capital goods within the country, plus any net addition to its overseas wealth as measured by any current account surplus over the period – or less any net disinvestment by the country in the form of a current account deficit. This broader objective will be termed 'thrift': for it represents the country's net saving over the period, whether that results in additions to its domestic stock of real capital wealth or its net holdings of claims on other countries.[1] This broader objective will be incorporated into the analysis of the latter part of the present chapter; for it is (as will be argued below) a more defensible policy objective than is the state of the current account of the balance of payments taken alone. But attention will be focused initially upon the state of the current account, because governments in fact place considerable weight on this objective – or at least on avoiding excessively large deficits, and sometimes also on avoiding excessively large surpluses. It will be seen from the empirical evidence in Chapter 6 that the combinations of macroeconomic policy measures that are appropriate if this is the focus of policy will often be different from those that are required if the third policy objective is the state of the current account taken alone.

The policy prescriptions that follow from a number of alternative assumptions about the relative effect of different macroeconomic instruments on these various objectives wll be discussed in Chapter 7, after empirical evidence has been assembled in Chapter 6 as to what appear to be the most reasonable assumptions to make about them. The present chapter raises *a priori* arguments relating to those considerations.

A PRIORI ARGUMENTS RELATING TO THE CURRENT ACCOUNT

The *a priori* arguments outlined in Chapter 2 relating to the closed economy also have relevance to the state of the current account; for, taken alone, the measures that have least upward effect on prices (for a given level or change in real output) are likely to be those that have the most favourable (or least unfavourable) effect on the current account – at least so far as the state of the current account depends on the competitiveness of the country's industries at any given nominal exchange rate. This being so, one would expect that a country with relatively low taxes and relatively low levels of government outlays relative to its total income or output would be more competitive (at any given nominal exchange rate) than one that had higher levels of either or both of these fiscal aggregates; and that a country that provided a real stimulus by increasing government outlays would therefore find its current account would deteriorate by more (for a given real stimulus) at any given nominal exchange rate than one that gave the same real stimulus by way of tax cuts.

The effects operating through the capital account must, however, also be considered (especially when we come to compare fiscal measures with changes in monetary policy). If the demand for money (in nominal terms) depends partly on the level, and rate of increase, in prices, then the form of stimulus that exerts the least upward (or the greatest downward) effect on prices would be the one that would do most to hold down the demand for capital inflow. In other words, one would expect that a stimulus provided by way of tax cuts would lead to a smaller rise in capital inflow, at least in nominal terms, than a rise in government outlays having the same effect on real output or employment – at any rate if one accepts the *a priori* arguments and empirical evidence of the preceding chapters.

In a world of generally floating exchange rates, one may view these two aspects of the effects of the different fiscal measures – through the current account and through the capital account – as two sides of the same coin. For the effect on the current account must in that case inevitably be balanced by an equivalent effect on the capital account. If a tax cut is the form of stimulus that has least upward effect on the current account deficit, then it must also – in a world of floating exchange rates – therefore be the form of fiscal stimulus that has least upward effect on capital inflow.

FISCAL VERSUS MONETARY MEASURES

The comparison between monetary measures, on the one hand, and all fiscal measures (taken together), on the other, has important aspects in the open economy. A fiscal stimulus (with the quantity of money held constant) tends to increase the rate of interest in the country giving the fiscal stimulus; and in a world of highly mobile flows of capital internationally and floating exchange rates this leads to increased net capital inflow (or reduced net capital outflow), to meet the increase in the demand for money, and thus to an appreciation of the currency of the country providing the fiscal stimulus – which increases the real quantity of money through its downward effect on prices. In the longer run, however, probably after several years, the addition to net income debits (or fall in net income credits) resulting from the country's additional interest payments on debts to residents of other countries (or the fall in its interest receipts from them) will tend to cause that currency to depreciate to some extent.

In contrast to the immediate effects of a *fiscal* stimulus, if the country had provided a *monetary* stimulus, this would operate in the direction of tending to *reduce* interest rates. In practice, however, rather than any great fall in interest rates, if international capital flows are very mobile one would expect the main effect to be a depreciation of the country's currency because of the consequent fall in the net inflow (or increase in the net outflow) of capital resulting from the rise in the supply of money, relative to the demand for it, at any given level of activity (compared with the situation that would have existed if the same real stimulus had been provided by a fiscal, instead of a monetary, measure).

This means that with a *monetary* stimulus, the effects on capital flows will be tending to reinforce the effects on the exchange rate that are operating through the current account when the macroeconomic stimulus is provided – as *both* those influences will be tending to *weaken* the currency in foreign exchange markets, and to that extent tending to improve the current account at any given level or rate of increase of real output or employment.

By contrast, for the reasons outlined above, with a *fiscal* stimulus the upward effect on net capital inflow tends to offset in part the tendency towards depreciation operating through the current account when the expansionary policies are adopted; so that the direction of the effect of a fiscal stimulus on the exchange rate is not clear *a priori*, though in a world of highly mobile capital flows, as the upward effect on capital inflow is likely to predominate, the net effect is likely to be in the direction of appreciation.

The implication of the preceding paragraphs is that if a monetary stimulus is employed it is likely to lead to a weaker currency – more depreciation – than if one of the forms of fiscal stimulus had been used. This may well be one of the main reasons why a monetary stimulus tends to have a greater upward effect on prices for any given real stimulus than do the fiscal measures (as the empirical evidence cited in Chapter 3 illustrated); for clearly a depreciation tends to raise the prices of traded goods (imports and exportables) in terms of the country's own currency, and to that extent exert upward pressure on its price level generally.

But that also means that a monetary measure of expansion will have a less unfavourable effect than a fiscal measure of expansion on the current account – and may even have a favourable effect. For the depreciation of the currency that results from the monetary expansion discourages imports and encourages exports; whereas with a fiscal expansion there will be much less depreciation, and may even be an appreciation, of the currency, which tends to encourage imports and discourage exports at any given level of activity. If, therefore, a country wishes to provide a stimulus in the form that has the least adverse effect on the current account (and which might have a favourable effect on it) that might appear to justify it in choosing a monetary stimulus rather than a fiscal one.

But monetary policy is in fact not a reliable instrument to use to try to influence the current account, with even the direction of its net effect being uncertain. For the two effects of monetary policy on the current account – the one tending to worsen any current account deficit through the stimulus it gives to domestic demand, and the other to improve it by causing depreciation of the currency at any given level of activity – tend to offset one another; and either of them may predominate, or the two may cancel one another out (as the empirical evidence in Chapter 6 will illustrate).

In any event, even if a tightening of monetary policy could be counted on to improve the current account, it could do so only by way of a greater sacrifice of potential output or employment (for a given improvement in the current account) than would result from a fiscal restraint – for which, as we have seen, the effects on the current account operating through the level of demand and through the exchange rate are pulling in the *same* direction. If the aim is to improve the current account balance with minimal loss of potential output or employment it is therefore fiscal measures of restraint that should be chosen – even if the government could be confident that a tightening of monetary policy would in fact operate in the direction of reducing a current account deficit (which, as we have seen above, it could not).

We also saw that, with a floating exchange rate, a change in the current account deficit is merely the obverse of a change in capital flows. A tightening of monetary policy must always be expected to tend to attract additional capital (at any given level of output or employment), and thus to lead to an increase in the current account deficit – balancing the additional net inflow of capital. Perhaps it is conceivable that a tightening of monetary policy could actually improve the current account (reduce net capital inflow) if the downward effect on aggregate demand greatly reduced the demand for capital from other countries; but, even then the same reduction in demand would presumably have the same downward effect on the demand for capital from other countries if it had resulted from fiscal contraction.

One other channel through which it might be suggested that a contractionary monetary policy could operate to reduce both capital inflow and the current account deficit would be if the rise in real interest rates resulting from tighter monetary policy leads to a sharp rise in the propensity to save (though changes in relative interest rates cannot usually go far in one individual country if there are highly mobile flows of capital to and from other countries). In any event, even the direction, and certainly the extent, of any such effect of interest changes upon the propensity to save has been the subject of much debate. It thus appears to be a very weak reed on which to lean in support of the hope that a tight monetary policy may improve a country's current account balance.

Any rise in real interest rates that a tighter monetary policy might bring about could exert direct downward presure on prices (at any given level of real output); and that might also in itself tend to improve the real state of the current account, and to reduce net capital inflow, by in effect increasing the *real* stock of money (for any given *nominal* stock of money).

But this could not be expected to lead to an actual rise in the real stock of money *compared with what it would have been in the absence of the monetary tightening*; for any downward pressure on prices would merely *reduce* the extent of the *fall* in the real stock of money when monetary policy was tightened – so that there would still be a net increase in the demand for capital inflow (at any given level of activity), and increased attraction for it, compared with the situation where the tightening of monetary policy had not occurred, and *a fortiori* compared with the situation where a tightening of fiscal policy had been used instead.

Why, then, have governments continued to use tighter monetary measures with the aim of improving the current account, even in a world of highly mobile flows of capital and floating exchange rates? One partial explanation might be that such thinking is a relic of the principles adopted in a world where exchange rates were generally fixed (at least in the short run) and capital flows were much less mobile internationally. Another might be that the governments concerned are simultaneously worried about excess demand, and are hoping that the adoption of tight monetary measures for that purpose will happen to operate also in the direction of reducing a current account deficit. In fact, however, in (at least) two countries that adopted successively tighter monetary measures in 1988–89 partly, at least, in an attempt to improve their current account – the UK and Australia – in both cases a powerful reason would appear to have been a reluctance to reverse expansionary fiscal measures in the forms of recent (or promised) tax cuts. But the fact that a measure (in this case a reversion to tighter fiscal measures) might have been politically awkward does not mean that it would have made any less economic sense.

The governments of some countries might hope that a tightening of monetary policy will tend to change the structure of the economy in an import-saving direction, if most of the capital goods required for investment purposes are imported. But an improvement in the current account that is brought about by an offsetting reduction in the stock of domestic capital is unlikely to constitute an overall improvement from the point of view of the country adopting the policy.

'THRIFT' AS AN OBJECTIVE

The state of the current account balance, even in the context of the country's accumulated creditor or debtor position, is thus inadequate as an objective. For example, if a government attempts to reduce a current account deficit by tight monetary measures (though these, as we saw above, may not even succeed in working towards that objective), this is likely to be at the expense of a reduction in the level of private investment. To improve a country's current account balance at the expense of a fully offsetting reduction in its additions to real productive wealth within the country will not increase its net wealth, and to that extent is unlikely to constitute any real macroeconomic improvement.

A far more appropriate objective is therefore the combined total of the addition to the country's stock of private capital plus any addition to its stock of overseas assets, by a current account surplus, or net of any reduction in its external wealth (increase in its external liabilities) resulting from a current account deficit. This is not to argue that it is always desirable to increase this total; for a country or its government may take the view that the sacrifice of consumption required to add one more unit to its stock of wealth is not worth accepting. But the basic argument remains that if a government is concerned to reduce the balance of payments deficit on current account it should not do so by adopting combinations of measures that will improve the current account only at the expense of bringing about an (at least) fully offsetting reduction in the country's stock of domestic productive capital. It will therefore be assumed in the rest of the analysis in this chapter that the third objective that is of concern to the government is the change in the total of domestic investment less any change in the current account in the direction of deficit (or plus any change in the direction of current account surplus). 'Thrift' appears to be an appropriate and simple name for this combined total, as it represents the level of the country's net saving (provided it is interpreted to include also the addition to the government's own stock of productively useful capital), whether it is used to finance additions to the country's stock of capital held within the country or that part held outside it.

This change to the consideration of this broader objective substantially enhances the *a priori* argument presented above relating to the use that should be made of monetary policy. It was argued in the earlier part of this chapter that monetary policy is an unreliable instrument to use with an eye to improving the current account (even the direction of its effect being uncertain). If the aim is to increase thrift, however, the argument for using an easing of monetary policy for this purpose is very strong, as this appears to be the macroeconomic instrument that has greatest effect on thrift (relative to its effects on other objectives, by comparison with those of the other macroeconomic instruments). This greatly reinforces the argument against using a *tightening* of monetary policy with the aim of trying to improve the current account; for it implies that even if this did improve the current account, the presumption is that it could be only at the expense of a more than offsetting reduction in the country's stock of privately owned capital, and therefore its level of thrift.

It may also reasonably be argued that cuts in certain types of government outlay can have an equally undesirable effect on the country's stock of domestic capital to those of a tightening of monetary policy; and that this too would constitute a reduction in thrift, so far as this element in that combined total is concerned. This does, indeed, constitute an important argument for making sure that cuts in government outlays are not concentrated (as they often have been) on the government's capital outlays. But one could at least be confident that even across-the-board cuts in government outlays would tend to improve the current account, and so to that extent to have a less adverse effect on thrift than a tightening of monetary policy having the same effect on the country's domestic stock of capital, but which will have a less favourable, or even an unfavourable, effect on the current account (for reasons discussed earlier in this chapter).

It is true that particular types of fiscal measures (subsidies or tax concessions) may be directed at stimulating or sustaining the country's total capital stock, whereas other types of fiscal measures may have most of their impact on consumption. We shall, however, in this analysis be considering only three policy instruments – wich may be thought of as comprising the typical (or 'average') form of government spending, the general level of taxation, and changes in monetary policy. In applying the analysis to actual policy decisions, however, one should bear in mind that the combination of assumptions about the effects of different instruments that are appropriate in any particular situation may change if one is confining attention to changes in, say, government *capital* outlays, or cuts in *indirect* taxes alone. (Some of the combinations of assumptions that will be discussed in Chapter 7 will be more appropriate to changes in particular types of tax or in particular types of government outlay, rather than to the average, or typical, tax or government outlay.)

Confining attention for the present, then, to government outlays generally, it would be reasonable to argue that if financed without the creation of money, they are more likely to crowd out private investment spending than are bond-financed tax cuts – some of which (at least) tend to improve the post-tax net return on investment (at any given level of total output or employment); while some forms of government outlay may replace productive activity that would otherwise have been undertaken by the private sector (at any given overall level or rate of increase in total real output or employment). Both tax cuts and government outlays will, however, tend to increase aggregate demand, including the level of many types of investment, if taken alone. The comparison being made here relates only to their *relative* effects on private investment for a given real stimulus. Government outlays may or may not crowd out (partly or wholly) some private investment that would otherwise have occurred at any given level of total real output; but they are far more likely to do so (or likely to encourage *less* additional private investment) than a tax cut having the same effect on real output or employment. Our *a priori* presumption will therefore be that a rise in government outlays may have an effect on thrift that is either (somewhat) favourable (though less so than a general tax cut) or unfavourable. For its adverse effect on the current account may be greater or less than any positive effect it may have on domestic investment, private and public). Tax cuts are also likely to have an unfavourable effect on the current account, but are more likely to have a net favourable effect (or a larger favourable effect) on private investment, and therefore probably also on total domestic investment, public plus private, unless the comparison being made is with a cut in government outlays *on capital works*. That favourable effect of tax cuts on private investment may or may not be sufficient to exceed the adverse effect of the tax cuts on the current account.

This leaves us with the clear *a priori* presumption about the ranking of the three broad macroeconomic instruments upon the objective of thrift: namely, that an easing of monetary policy is most likely to increase thrift (for any given real stimulus to total output or employment), whereas tax cuts are more likely to have a favourable effect on thrift than is the typical form of government outlay (or less likely to have an unfavourable effect on it). It may be observed that this ranking is different from that discussed in Chapters 2 and 3 relating to their respective effects on prices. The presumption argued on *a priori* grounds in Chapter 2 (and evidenced by the empirical material in Chapter 3) was that an easing of monetary policy was the most inflationary (and therefore the *least* desirable form of stimulus from that point of view), whereas if thrift is the principal other macroeconomic objective, an easing of monetary policy scores most highly (assuming that the aim is to increase thrift). If the comparison is between different fiscal instruments, on the other hand, tax cuts generally score more highly than increases in government outlays, whether the aim is to minimise the extent to which a real stimulus increases prices or to minimise the adverse effects of the stimulus on the current account (or on thrift).

In the following chapters these principles and their implications for policy will be illustrated by empirical evidence from econometric models (in Chapter 6) and by simplified numerical examples (in Chapter 7).

NOTE

1. I owe this usage of the term 'thrift' to Ian McDonald, who convinced me that it was both useful and apposite in this context.

6 The Mix in the Open Economy: Some Empirical Evidence

This chapter brings together a number of pieces of evidence from the econometric models that were used in Chapter 3, to throw light on the relative effects of different macroeconomic policy measures on the current account of the balance of payments, for a given effect on real output.

The arguments outlined in the previous chapter raised the *a priori* presumption that, for a given upward effect on real output or employment, an easing of monetary policy would have the least unfavourable effect on the current account (and might even have a favourable effect) in a world of generally floating exchange rates; and that government outlays would tend to have a more unfavourable effect (again, for a given real stimulus) than a tax cut.

As we saw in Chapter 5, governments ought generally to be concerned to ensure that any measures they take to improve the current account of the balance of payments are not of a sort that would have a (fully offsetting) downward effect on useful forms of productive investment within the country. For an improvement in the country's international net debtor/creditor position (a reduction in the current account deficit or increase in the current account surplus) that is brought about only with a fully offsetting reduction in the level of its productive forms of domestic investment is very unlikely to constitute an increase in the country's net wealth. Any such repercussions – positive or negative – of alternative measures on the level of private investment ought therefore also to be taken into account.

In particular, an expansionary monetary policy is likely to have a greater upward effect on private investment (for a given real stimulus or for any adverse effect it may have on the current account balance) than are typical fiscal measures. At any rate, this is likely to be true provided that the tax cuts or government outlays in question are not specifically directed at encouraging investment. If this is taken into account, therefore, the margin of advantage from using fiscal measures of restraint to improve the current account, rather than a tightening of monetary policy, would be enhanced.

On the other hand, an expansionary fiscal measure may also have some favourable effects on private investment; and, if this is so, that favourable effect should be deducted from any adverse effect on the current account balance that results when that fiscal instrument is moved in an expansionary direction; for that would give a measure of the effect of that change in policy upon the country's total domestic private investment plus (or minus) any change in its net overseas investment (in the shape of a change in the net current account balance)– hereafter to be termed 'thrift'. For completeness, any change in the government's own capital investment ought also to be brought into the calculation; but we shall here ignore this consideration, in effect making the assumption that the government's outlays that are being increased or reduced are not on capital goods.

Similarly, if a fiscal measure of expansion has an adverse effect on private investment, that effect ought to be added to the likely adverse effect of these measures upon the current account – if a government is trying to assess the likely effect on the country's thrift.

Table 6.1 shows that for all seven major OECD countries measures of monetary expansion have a negligible effect on the real current account balance, and that any small effect there may be is for some countries slightly positive and for others slightly negative, taking the average *level* for the five-year period as a whole. The figures for the average year-to-year change over the five-year period as a whole show that by the end of the five-year period any effect on the real current account balance has disappeared except for the US (for which it is slightly positive) and the UK and Japan (for which it is slightly negative).

Table 6.1 also shows that for all seven major OECD countries, both a rise in government outlays and a cut in income tax rates (whether with money or interest rates held constant) would have an adverse effect on the real foreign balance; but that, for each of these countries, with an income tax cut the adverse effect would be less per unit of stimulus to real GNP/GDP than with a rise in government outlays financed in the same way. Each of these fiscal measures has a more adverse effect on the real value of the current account balance with money held constant than the same measure with an accommodating monetary policy (one that holds interest rates constant), taking the average of the five years after the change of policy. (Taking the change from the beginning to the end of the five-year period, there are some cases where, with interest rates held constant, these two fiscal measures

Table 6.1 Effects of alternative measures on change in real foreign balance for 1 per cent stimulus to real GDP, with floating exchange rates, seven major OECD countries (change in annual average level over five years as per cent of base GNP/GDP, with average annual change over the period in parentheses)

	US	*Japan*	*West Germany*	*France*	*UK*	*Italy*	*Canada*
Cut in short-term interest	−0.03 (+0.02)	−0.02 (−0.05)	0.00 (0.00)	+0.19 (0.00)	−0.09 (−0.03)	+0.11 (0.00)	0.00 (0.00)
Cut in income tax interest rates constant	−0.23 (−0.05)	−0.18 (−0.06)	−0.46 (−0.11)	−0.38 (−0.07)	−0.51 (−0.10)	−0.36 (−0.07)	−0.47 (−0.09)
Rise in government outlays, interest rates constant	−0.40 (−0.09)	−0.24 (−0.06)	−0.49 (−0.15)	−0.40 (−0.07)	−0.57 (−0.11)	−0.40 (−0.10)	−0.48 (−0.10)
Cut in income tax, money constant	−0.38 (−0.13)	−0.42 (−0.40)	−0.77 (−0.23)	−0.51 (−0.13)	−0.80 (−0.25)	−0.39 (−0.09)	−0.90 (−0.50)
Ris in government outlays. money constant	−0.73 (−0.30)	−0.57 *	−0.83 (−0.28)	−0.64 (−0.18)	−0.96 (−0.33)	−0.49 (−0.13)	−1.04 *

* These figures are undefined, as this measure gives no stimulus to real output by Year 5 for Japan and Canada.

SOURCE: derived from Richardson, 1987 and 1988 and data supplied by him.

have virtually the same effect on the real value of the current account balance by the end of the period for a given real stimulus.)

Table 6.2 shows that these simulations suggest that, as the use of a monetary measure of expansion always has also a favourable effect on private investment, it thus has a favourable effect on thrift; whereas, for a given upward effect on real GNP/GDP, all the forms of fiscal expansion had either an unfavourable, or a much smaller favourable, effect on thrift than a purely monetary measure of expansion.

Table 6.2 also shows that, with money held constant, a cut in income

Table 6.2 Effect of alternative measures on change in thrift (private investment plus or minus change in real foreign balance) for one per cent stimulus to real GNP/GDP, with floating exchange rates, seven major OECD countries (change in annual average level over five years as per cent of base GNP/GDP, with average annual change over the period in parentheses)

	US	*Japan*	*West Germany*	*France*	*UK*	*Italy*	*Canada*
Cut in short-term interest rates	+0.84 (+0.11)	+0.83 (+0.05)	+0.52 (+0.10)	+1.02 (+0.17)	+0.93 (−0.12)	+2.01 (+0.13)	+0.54 (+0.11)
Cut in income tax, interest rates constant	+0.58 (+0.04)	+0.33 (+0.04)	+0.01 (−0.06)	+0.23 (−0.04)	−0.12 (−0.01)	+0.25 (+0.01)	+0.04 (+0.05)
Rise in government outlays, interest rates constant	−0.03 (+0.03)	+0.19 (+0.03)	−0.16 (−0.08)	+0.06 (+0.04)	−0.18 (−0.01)	+0.03 (+0.01)	−0.06 (+0.05)
Cut in income tax, money constant	−0.24 (−0.27)	−0.33 (−0.26)	−0.35 (−0.15)	+0.03 (−0.02)	−0.84 (−0.37)	+0.14 (−0.17)	−0.20 (−0.36)
Rise in government outlays, money constant	−0.83 (−0.41)	−1.01 *	−0.67 (−0.24)	−0.34 (−0.08)	−1.18 (−0.07)	−0.27 (−0.12)	−0.72 *

* These figures are undefined, as this measure has no effect on real output by year 5 for these two countries.
NOTE: original data for effect on private investment are expressed as a per cent of base private investment. Here those results are converted to a percentage of GNP/GDP by using the ratio of gross private fixed capital investment to GDP in 1985, from OECD *Historical Statistics*.
SOURCE: derived from Richardson, 1987 and 1988 and data supplied by him.

tax again had a less unfavourable effect on thrift than a rise in government outlays (or in some cases a favourable effect when outlays had an unfavourable one).

The same broad conclusions follow when interest rates are held constant in the face of expansionary fiscal measures: the cut in income tax always scores better than the rise in government outlays in terms of its effects on the average level of thrift over the five years. As a stimulus of this sort is midway between a monetary expansion (a cut in short-term interest rates in these simulations) and a fiscal expansion with money held constant, it is not surprising that the effects of a given fiscal change on thrift (as also those on the current account) are intermediate between those of a monetary stimulus and those of the same fiscal stimulus with money held constant.

More often than not, income tax cuts with interest rates held constant have a favourable effect on thrift (on either of the statistical measurements given in Table 6.2) – the exceptions being the UK (marginally) for the five-year average level and France, West Germany and the UK for the average annual change over the course of the period. Government outlays (with interest held constant) have a downward effect on thrift in a majority of the countries over the five-year average, though in only two of them for the change over the whole period.

As the different fiscal measures have different effects on the average level of thrift over the five years (as also on the current account taken alone) for a given real stimulus, there are clearly combinations of fiscal measures that can be used to increase real output without an adverse effect on thrift (or on the current account, or both). In particular, there are clearly combinations of tax cuts and reductions in government outlays that can be used to raise real output (with the quantity of money held constant, or, alternatively, with an accommodating monetary policy) to give a stimulus to real output without bringing about a net adverse effect on the real foreign balance or thrift. In order to do this it must be given by way of the fiscal measure with the less adverse effect (or the greater favourable effect) on the current account (or on thrift), with the other fiscal measure being operated in a contractionary direction, if necessary, to an appropriate extent. Clearly no contractionary adjustment of another measure would be needed if a form of stimulus is used that has a net favourable effect on thrift (or the current account), even taken by itself.

For several of these countries a stimulus could be provided without a worsening of the current account by a combination of measures that included a monetary expansion. But this evidence from the OECD simulations shows that, for all countries except Canada, monetary expansion has a much greater upward effect on prices (per unit of real stimulus) than any of these forms of fiscal expansion; so that if the country in question is concerned to hold down prices as well as to give a real stimulus with minimal adverse effect on private investment and the current account, it will not necessarily be well advised to use a monetary stimulus merely because it has the largest favourable effect on thrift – unless, of course, the consequently greater upward pressure on prices is not a matter of serious concern to the government.

This being so, it is important for a country that also wishes to hold down prices to know whether there are combinations of the fiscal instruments, or of fiscal instruments together with monetary policy) that will give a non-inflationary stimulus while improving the current account or also giving a stimulus to thrift – or at least avoiding any adverse effect on these. There are a range of combinations of income tax cuts that could, on the evidence of these OECD simulations, be combined with a reduction in government outlays in such a way as to give a non-inflationary stimulus. We need now to enquire whether or not those combinations of reductions in government outlays and income tax cuts will tend also to have a favourable effect on the real foreign balance or on thrift.

Table 6.3 shows the range of income tax cuts that can be combined with a reduction in government outlays equal to one per cent of GDP to give a non-inflationary stimulus in each of these countries, with a

Table 6.3 Combinations of income tax cuts with reductions of government outlays equal to 1 per cent of GNP/GDP to give non-inflationary stimulus, with floating exchange rates and fixed quantity of money, seven major OECD countries (annual average over five years as per cent of base GNP/GDP)

	US	*Japan*	*West Germany*	*France*	*UK*	*Italy*	*Canada*
Total range	0.9 to 1.24	1.06 to 1.29	1.00 to 1.40	1.15 to 1.86	1.08 to 2.17	1.08 to 1.61	1.29 to 1.81
of which							
Range with constant or improving real foreign balance	0.9 to 1.24	1.06 to 1.29	1.00 to 1.07	1.15 to 1.45	1.08 to 1.30	1.08 to 1.33	None
Range with constant or increasing 'thrift'*	0.9 to 1.24	1.06 to 1.29	1.00 to 1.07	1.15 to 1.45	None	1.08 to 1.33	1.29 to 1.47

* Private investment plus any improvement or less any deterioration in real foreign balance.

SOURCE: derived from Richardson, 1987 and 1988 and data supplied by him.

constant quantity of money; and also the range of these income tax cuts that will give a non-inflationary stimulus without worsening the real foreign balance. The table also shows that for all these countries except the UK there is a range of income tax cuts that would, on the same assumptions, give a non-inflationary stimulus without having an adverse effect on thrift.

Furthermore, Table 6.3 shows that those simulations also imply that in all these countries except Canada there is a range of income tax cuts that could be combined with a reduction in government outlays to give a non-inflationary stimulus without worsening the real foreign balance; and that for all these countries except the UK that would also be consistent with avoiding a fall in thrift.

Table 6.4 shows a more detailed working of these calculations for the US, partly to show the method of calculation, and partly because of the importance to the world generally, and not only to the US, of knowing whether or not there are combinations of fiscal measures that can provide a non-inflationary stimulus in the US while still improving the US balance of payments on current account. The results cast considerable doubt on the justification for the constantly re-iterated advice to the US to reduce its budget deficit *in order to* reduce its current account deficit.

The table shows that (so far as the OECD simulations for the US show) alternative combinations of changes in government outlays and income tax in the US would be possible that would either (i) lead to an *improvement* in the fiscal balance with a *deterioration* of the real foreign balance or (ii) lead to a *deterioration* of the fiscal balance with an *improvement* in the real foreign balance.

This emphasises that the 'twin deficits' approach – which argues that a reduction in the fiscal deficit is necessary in order to achieve a reduction in the current account deficit – is highly misleading; for the above figures illustrate that a reduction in the fiscal deficit is neither a sufficient nor a necessary condition for an improvement in the current account balance.

Indeed, if an attempt is made to reduce the fiscal balance by a combination of measures that includes a rise in government outlays together with a rise in income taxes sufficient to bring about a reduction in the fiscal deficit, these figures suggest that only if the tax increase were sufficient to reduce the fiscal deficit by nearly 0.9 % of GNP would this result in a fall in the real foreign deficit, and that in the process it would lead to a net fall of 0.7 % in GNP. (A balanced budget increase of government outlays and income taxes would, on these figures lead to a fall in real GNP.)

Table 6.4 Effects of alternative fiscal measures in the US, with floating exchange rates and fixed quantity of money (change in five-year annual average)

	Effects on			
	Real GNP (%)	*GDP price index (%)*	*Fiscal balance* (% of base GNP)	*Real foreign balance* (% of base GNP)
Policy change (% of GNP)				
Rise in government outlays (1%)	0.66	1.52	−1.14	−0.48
Income tax cut (1%)	0.74	1.22	−1.08	−0.28
Rise in government outlays (1%)	+0.66	+1.52	−1.14	−0.48
Rise in income tax (1.1%)	−0.81	−1.34	+1.16	+0.31
Both the above	−0.15	+0.18	+0.02	−0.17
Cut in government outlays (1%)	−0.66	−1.52	+1.14	+0.48
Income tax cut (1.6%)	+1.18	+1.96	−1.78	−0.46
Both the above	+0.52	+0.44	−0.64	+0.02

SOURCE: derived from Richardson, 1987 and 1988 and data supplied by him.

If the movement towards reducing the external deficit was by way of reductions in both income tax and government outlays, however, by reversing the signs in the preceding example it may be seen that a cut in government outlays equal to 1% of GNP combined with a cut in income tax equal to under 1.7% of GNP could bring about an *improvement* in the current account balance, though with a substantial *increase* in the fiscal *deficit* – and a substantial net stimulus to real GNP. This emphasises how attempts to reduce the external deficit by reducing the fiscal deficit may rule out combinations of these two fiscal measures that could improve the external deficit without reducing (and, indeed, even while actually increasing) real output.

If simulations were available for the US of other types of tax cut, notably cuts in indirect taxes, one might reasonably suppose that – on the basis of the results for the EEC reported in a later section – it would be even more likely that an improvement in the current account could be brought about by combinations of measures (including cuts in indirect taxes) that would not reduce the fiscal deficit; and that reductions in the fiscal deficit that were brought about by way of *increases* in indirect taxes would not necessarily reduce the external deficit, and might be expected to reduce real output and exert upward pressure on prices.

EVIDENCE FROM SIMULATIONS WITH UK MODELS

Table 6.5 shows that simulations at the University of Warwick with the four main quarterly models of the UK economy indicate that, on

Table 6.5 Effect of alternative macroeconomic measures on UK current account balance for 1 percent rise in real GDP (change in average annual level of current account over five years as per cent of base GDP)

Stimulus	*Model LBS*	*NIESR*	*HMT*	*B of E*	*Average*
Cut in short-term interest rates	−0.72	−0.08	−0.18	+0.30	−0.17
Cut in income tax*	−0.67	−0.29	−0.66	−0.17	−0.45
Cut in VAT*	−0.79	−0.43	−0.51	−0.17	−0.48
Cut in employers' national insurance contributions*	−0.52	−0.40	−0.42	−0.12	−0.36
Rise in government outlays*	−0.73	−0.35	−0.53	−0.22	−0.46
Rise in government outlays with money fixed	−0.96	−0.44	−1.98	−0.26	−0.91

* Signifies 'with interest rates held constant'.
LBS = London Business School; NIESR = National Institute of Economic and Social Research; HMT = Her Majesty's Treasury; B of E = Bank of England.
SOURCE: derived from Fisher *et al*, 1988.

the average of the following five years, of the measures of macroeconomic stimulus that were simulated in these tests, a cut in short-term interest rates has the smallest adverse effect on the current account for a given stimulus to real output in two of the four models, and, in one model, even a positive effect on the current account. In the remaining model, two of the tax cuts simulated (with interest rates held constant), as well as an accommodated rise in government outlays, have a less adverse effect on the current account (per unit of stimulus to real GNP) than does a monetary expansion.

But in all four models a rise in government outlays with money held constant had the largest adverse effect on the current account (for a given real stimulus) among the measures tested (all the other fiscal measures being tested with interest rates held constant). In three models a cut in employers' national insurance contributions had a less adverse effect on the current account than the other measures. Thus if a cut in government outlays, with money held constant, were accompanied by an appropriate cut in income tax (all models) or by a cut in VAT or in employers' national insurance contributions (each in three of the models), with *interest rates* held constant, these figures suggest that it would be possible to provide a real stimulus with a simultaneous improvement in the current account.

Over the average for the five-year period, in three of the four models a tightening of monetary policy would be the worst way (in terms of the amount of real output that would have to be forgone) among those tested to achieve a given improvement in the current account of the balance of payments (and in one model it would actually worsen the current account). In every model it would be clearly less efficient for this purpose than a cut in government outlays with money held constant. In three of the four models it would also be inferior to a rise in employers' national insurance contributions and also inferior to a rise in VAT or to a cut in government outlays with interest rates held constant. Reductions in government outlays (with money held constant) could thus (on this evidence) be combined with one or more of these alternative forms of fiscal stimulus in such a way as to increase real output without worsening the current account.

Trying to improve the current account by tight monetary policy would also be inferior to an accommodated rise in VAT in all four models and to an accommodated rise in employers' national insurance contributions in three of them; so that some combination of an easing of monetary policy with a rise in VAT, and perhaps a rise in employers' national insurance contributions, would be another way of bringing about a net improvement in the current account.

It was shown in Table 6.1 that the results of the OECD simulations indicated (consistently with the balance of the results for the UK given in Table 6.5) that, of the measures simulated by them, tight monetary policy was the worst way of trying to improve the current account, not only in terms of the fall in real output needed if it were to succeed, but also in the sense that for the UK it would not (on those simulations, as also for the Warwick test using the Bank of England model) improve the current account at all on the average of the five years. On the OECD simulations also, it was seen that of the measures tested in their model a cut in government outlays with money held constant had the greatest effect in improving the UK's current account for a given decline in real output (that is, a smaller fall in real output was needed to effect a given improvement in the current account) than with any of the other measures tested. This was also true of three of the four UK models.

The conclusions about the UK that can be derived from the OECD simulations can thus be used to complement the Warwick tests – which assume that interest rates are held constant when fiscal measures are employed (except for one set of simulations of a rise in government outlays).

The OECD conclusions are generally consistent with the balance of the evidence from the tests using the UK models, so far as the two sets of results can be compared with one another – that is, so far as they relate to cuts in interest rates, to bond-financed government outlays, and to accommodated cuts in income tax or accommodated rises in government outlays. But the OECD simulation results imply also that if a rise in income tax rates or a cut in government outlays was employed to try to improve the current account, it would be better to hold money constant than to keep interest rates fixed; and that a cut in government outlays would be preferable to a rise in income tax financed in the same way if either of these instruments were to be used to try to improve the current account with a minimum loss of real output.

EVIDENCE FROM EEC SIMULATIONS

Table 6.6 shows that simulations done with the EEC COMPACT model (Dramais, 1986) of alternative forms of bond-financed stimulus had varying effects on the current account balance of the EEC as a whole, for any given effect on real GDP.

Cuts in income tax had an only slightly less adverse effect on the current account than did rises in government outlays for a given effect

Table 6.6 Effects of alternative fiscal measures on the current account balance and on private investment in the EEC for 1 per cent rise in real GDP (change in average annual level over five years as per cent of base GDP, with average annual change over five years in parentheses)

	Change in current account	*Change in private investment*	*Change in private investment less rise in current account deficit*
Cut in employers' social security contributions	−0.22 (−0.03)	+0.45 (+0.03)	+0.23 (0.00)
Cut in household indirect taxes	−0.25 (−0.04)	+0.23 (+0.03)	−0.02 (−0.01)
Cut in household direct taxes	−0.47 (−0.11)	+0.21 (+0.04)	−0.26 (−0.07)
Rise in public investment	−0.50 (−0.16)	+0.15 (−0.03)	−0.35 (−0.19)

NOTE: figures for private investment, which are expressed as a percentage of baseline investment in the original, have here been converted to a per cent of GDP using the ratio of Gross Private Fixed Capital Formation to GDP in 1986 from OECD, *Historical Statistics.*
SOURCE: derived from Dramais, 1986.

on real GDP, but the other two types of tax cut simulated had a much less adverse effect (indeed, only about half as great) over the average of the five years after the introduction of the measure than did a rise in government outlays. The main difference in the relative effects on the current account is thus between government outlays or cuts in income tax, on the one hand, and cuts in employers' social security contributions or in value-added tax, on the other.

The policy conclusion from these results must therefore be that there are combinations of reductions in government outlays and in taxes (even if these were cuts in income taxes), with money held constant, that would improve the current account at any given level of activity; and, indeed, even in the face of a non-inflationary stimulus. One such combination would be a reduction of government outlays of a given order of magnitude, accompanied by a cut in either household indirect taxes, or in employers' social security contributions (or some combination of the two) equivalent to slightly more than half the value of the cut in government outlays. Another would be to accompany the cut in government outlays by a somewhat smaller cut in income tax receipts.

As Table 6.6 shows, the evidence from the EEC simulations (which relates only to fiscal measures of stimulus, and with money held constant – in effect, each fiscal stimulus being bond-financed – suggests that the ranking of these four instruments is the same in terms of their respective effects on the average level of the current account as for their effects on private investment (for a given stimulus to real GDP). A cut in employers' social security contributions is the only one of these measures that has such a large upward effect on private investment as to exceed its unfavourable effect on the current account balance (its adverse effect on which is the least of the four); a cut in indirect taxes has more or less the same upward effect on private investment (per unit of stimulus to real GDP) as does a cut in household direct taxes; but the cut in indirect taxes, as well as having a slightly more favourable effect on private investment than cuts in household direct taxes, has a much less adverse effect on the current account. Government outlays (in this simulation described as 'public investment' – though the source makes it clear that the model does not permit the effects of this form of public spending on goods and services to be differentiated from those of other forms) clearly has the greatest adverse effect on the current account and the least favourable effect on private investment of the four forms of fiscal stimulus that have been simulated by the EEC.

Taking together the effects upon private investment and on the current account balance (together termed 'thrift') of each of these fiscal measures, and comparing their effects with that on the current account taken by itself, it may be seen that government outlays – which were only marginally the form of stimulus that had the most adverse effect on the current account – are the measure that had clearly the most adverse effect on thrift. A cut in household direct tax, which had nearly as great an adverse effect on the current account as did a rise in government outlays having the same effect on real output, had an appreciably smaller adverse effect on thrift than did government outlays.

A cut in indirect taxes, which had only a slightly more adverse effect on the current account than did a cut in employers' social security contributions, had a small adverse effect on thrift; and a cut in employers' social security contributions had a very marked positive effect on the combined total, in contrast to its clearly adverse effect on the current account.

If one looks at the average year-to-year *change* from the beginning to the end of the five-year period (rather than that in the average *level* over the five years), the ranking of these measures is not substantially different. But on this criterion the cut in indirect taxes now scores best in terms of its effect on thrift (which is now slightly positive) or on the current account taken alone. The rise in government outlays still has the greatest adverse effect on the current account alone or on thrift, with a cut in household direct taxes being superior to a rise in government outlays, but inferior to the two other measures tested.

A NON-INFLATIONARY STIMULUS AND THE CURRENT ACCOUNT

The EEC simulations imply that there are various combinations of tax cuts with reductions in government outlays that can be used to give a non-inflationary stimulus; and that, even taken alone, a cut in employers' social security contributions not only gives a non-inflationary stimulus to output, but (to judge from these results) does not have an unfavourable effect on the total of private investment less any rise in the current account deficit (though it tends to worsen the current account balance taken by itself).

Let us take first the combination of a cut in government outlays equal to one per cent of GDP and a simultaneous reduction in income tax sufficient to give a non-inflationary stimulus. As Table 6.7 shows, the extent to which (according to the results of this simulation) household direct tax would need to be cut in order to give a non-inflationary stimulus by this combination of measures would leave a substantial net favourable effect on the current account or on thrift. This can be seen from the figure in the line for cuts in household direct taxes relating to the average effect over the five years on the current account, or on the total for private investment less any rise in the current account deficit – figures that are substantially less adverse than the corresponding (positive) ones for a cut in government outlays.

Moreover, if the cut in government outlays equal to one per cent of GDP were combined with either of the other two types of tax cut there is also a range of combinations with these tax cuts that would provide a non-inflationary stimulus without a deterioration of the current account and without a reduction in thrift. For in each case the table

Table 6.7 Effects on private investment and the current account of alternative forms of fiscal stimulus in the EEC (change in average annual level over five years as per cent of base GDP, with average annual change over the five years in parentheses)

	Effect on				
Change (as % of base GDP)	*(1) current account*	*(2) private investment*	*(3) (1)+(2)*	*Real GDP*	*GDP price index*
	(% of base GDP)			*(%)*	*(%)*
Cut in government outlays (1%)	+0.44 (+0.08)	−0.13 (+0.02)	+0.31 (+0.10)	−0.88 (−0.10)	−0.88 (−0.34)
Cut in household direct tax (1.5%)	−0.42 (−0.12)	+0.19 (+0.05)	−0.23 (−0.07)	+0.90 (+0.21)	+0.72 (+0.30)
Cut in household indirect tax (0.9% of GDP)	−0.23 (−0.04)	+0.21 (+0.05)	−0.02 (+0.01)	+0.92 (+0.20)	−0.92 (−0.14)
Reduction in employers' social security contributions (1% of GDP)	−0.20 (−0.04)	+0.40 (+0.16)	+0.20 (+0.12)	+0.90 (+0.30)	−1.02 (−0.28)

SOURCE: derived from Dramais, 1986.

shows that the adverse effect on the current account of the tax cuts in question is much less than the favourable effect of the cut in government outlays (for the same effect on real output); and that the upward effect on private investment of the tax cuts exceeds the downward effect on investment of the cut in government outlays.

The last two columns of the table show that in each case the tax cuts of the order shown increase real GDP by more than it is reduced by a cut in government outlays equal to one per cent of GDP; and that the net effect on prices of the cut in government outlays coupled with tax cuts of the order shown is in each case downwards.

The tax cuts illustrated in Table 6.7 are in each case about the minimum that would have a favourable effect on all the objectives (assuming the aim is to reduce the current account deficit and raise real output without raising prices). Clearly, much bigger cuts in employers' social security contributions or in household indirect taxes would have a helpful effect on all these objectives; only if the cuts in either of those taxes were equal to at least two per cent of GDP would the provision of a further non-inflationary stimulus in this way bring about a net deterioration in the current account. Any cut in household direct taxes appreciably larger than that shown in the table would, however, bring about a net deterioration in the current account.

If a comparison is made of the effects over the course of the whole five-year period (in effect, comparing the situation at the end of that period with what it would have been in the absence of the policy change), cuts in these taxes of the order shown in the table, together with a cut in government outlays equal to one per cent of GDP, could still be expected to give a non-inflationary stimulus. But the table also shows that by the end of the period cuts in household direct taxes of the order shown would lead to a rise in the current account deficit, though not to a net adverse effect on thrift. A smaller cut in household direct taxes (equal to only one per cent of GDP) with a cut in government outlays of the same order would, however, still leave a non-inflationary stimulus, without a worsening of the current account. Cuts in the other taxes of the order shown, with the same reduction in government outlays, would continue to have favourable net effects on all the objectives at the end of the five-year period.

Table 6.7 shows the minimum cuts in each of these three different types of taxes that would, in combination with a reduction in government outlays equal to one per cent of GDP, leave a net rise in real output without upward pressure on the price level.

It may be seen that the increase in the current account deficit resulting from the minimum tax cut needed to provide a net real stimulus in the face of this reduction in government outlays is in each case less than the improvement in the current account balance resulting from the reduction in government outlays; so that the minimum tax cut required to provide a real non-inflationary stimulus (coupled with that reduction in government spending) also has a net favourable effect on the current account balance as well as on thrift.

There is a range of tax cuts of which this is true. But it may also be seen that for cuts in employers' social security contributions or in household indirect taxes, there is a range of tax cuts that can be coupled with a cut in government outlays to give a non-inflationary stimulus but with a net *upward* effect on any current account deficit (or downward effect on any current account surplus). This is obviously an important conclusion when a country has an excessive structural current account surplus; for it means that there are combinations of fiscal measures

Table 6.8 Effects on the EEC current account of alternative combinations of tax cuts with reductions in government outlays equal to 1 per cent of GDP (change in annual average of five years after the change as per cent of base GDP)

Range of tax cuts (as per cent of GDP) that will give non-inflationary stimulus with stated effect on current account balance

	To keep current account constant	*To reduce current account deficit*	*To reduce current account surplus*
Cut in household direct tax	1.6	1.5 to 1.6	1.6 to 1.8
Cut in employers' social security contributions	2.2	1.0 to 2.2	More than 2.2
Cut in household indirect taxes	1.7	0.9 to 1.6	More than 1.6

SOURCE: derived from Dramais, 1986.
NOTE: all the measures tested assume that the quantity of money is held constant.

available that will help to solve this problem *without the need for such countries to introduce inflationary forms of fiscal stimulus.* In that case, such a country would be able to reduce its current account surplus by appropriate forms of fiscal policy, even though at the same time holding domestic real output constant or even reducing it (see Table 6.8).

CONCLUSIONS

The results of these simulations (coming as they do from a variety of sources and models) afford strong evidence that there are not merely combinations of macroeconomic instruments that can give a non-inflationary stimulus – indeed, ones that can stimulate real output or employment while also exerting *downward* pressure on prices (at least over a five-year period) – but that such combinations are often also ones that will tend to improve the balance on current account. If a country feels inhibited from taking expansionary action (when it has unemployed resources) merely by fears that a stimulatory policy must inevitably exert upward pressure on prices or have adverse effects on the current account, therefore, a choice of appropriate combinations of two or more macroeconomic instruments will (on this evidence) generally be available to enable it to set those qualms at rest. On the other hand, there are also combinations of measures that will, on this evidence, provide a non-inflationary stimulus but which would at the same time tend to reduce a current account surplus.

It may be argued that if a tightening of monetary policy is one of the measures used to restrain prices, most of its effect operates through the exchange rate, and will to that extent be operating in a manner that exports to other countries the inflationary pressures that the country tightening its monetary policy is seeking to reduce. If, however, that is felt to be a sufficient objection to a mix of tighter monetary policy coupled with fiscal expansion, there are other combinations, of reductions in government outlays combined with certain types of tax cuts (and probably with *any* types of tax cut), that will achieve the same aim of providing a non-inflationary stimulus without relying on the exchange rate as their channel of operation, and often with net favourable effects (or at least no adverse effect) on the current account.

The alternative of changing the mix *within* fiscal policy (rather than as between fiscal and monetary measures) has the additional advantage that the use of a tightening of monetary policy to reduce inflation would have been likely also to have adverse effects on the level of private investment at any given level of activity. If this consideration is felt to be important, and if it is therefore added to the presumption that a tightening of monetary policy will have only a small effect – even the direction of which is uncertain – on the current account, this means that appropriate changes *within* the fiscal mix are more appropriate for a country that is concerned to maintain the ratio of private investment to GDP (or to avoid reducing the total of private investment less any rise in the current account deficit) than a change in mix that includes a tightening of monetary policy.

At any given time one might hope that there will be as many countries concerned to try to reduce an excessive current account surplus as to reduce an external deficit. For if there is on balance more concern on the part of governments to reduce external deficits than surpluses, the net effect will be downward pressure on demand in the world economy; for the totality of efforts to improve the current account of the balance of payments would in that case bring about a net deflationary effect. On the other hand, if the majority of governments were trying to increase their current account deficits, that would be tending to cause excess demand in the world economy.

If, however, at any given time, the state of the current account of some countries is thought to be excessively strong, on a scale that approximately balances the extent to which other countries believe theirs to be excessively weak, it should thus not be thought to be a general disadvantage if the combinations of measures most likely to provide a non-inflationary stimulus happened to be also ones that tended to worsen the current account. Ideally, one would hope that there would be some forms of non-inflationary stimulus that could be used by countries wishing also to reduce their external deficits on current account, and other forms of non-inflationary stimulus that could be used by countries with excessive external surpluses while reducing those surpluses. It is thus of special interest and importance that the evidence discussed above implies that, for some countries at any rate, there appear to be some combinations of different fiscal instruments that will tend to provide a non-inflationary stimulus and also have a favourable effect on the current acount; and that for many countries there is also a different range of these or other combinations of fiscal instruments that would give a non-inflationary stimulus while tending to reduce an excessive current account surplus.

Moreover, the combinations of measures that will provide a non-inflationary stimulus will not necessarily involve an increase in a country's fiscal deficit; so that if fears that this may occur are inhibiting a government from taking expansionary action, this need not necessarily be a barrier. At the very least, the equating in so many people's minds of the provision of a fiscal stimulus with a movement of the fiscal balance towards greater (structural) deficit is not defensible. It also appears to be true that combinations of fiscal measures that will tend to improve the current account balance may not necessarily be ones that will tend also to reduce the fiscal deficit – especially if they are also to be combinations that will help to stimulate the level of employment and real output while holding down the price level. By the same token, some combinations of measures that would tend to reduce the fiscal deficit would not tend to improve the current account balance. This being so, the so-called 'twin-deficit' approach is not merely unhelpful, but it may very often lead to the adoption of measures that will make the external problem worse, even if they reduce the fiscal deficit; and it may also lead to combinations of measures that will tend to reduce real output or employment (for any given degree of upward pressure on prices), or to bring about a greater degree of upward pressure on prices for any given level or rate of increase in real output or employment.

Just as changes in the fiscal balance are no guide to whether policy is being moved in an expansionary direction when different fiscal measures have different effects on real output or employment for a given effect on the fiscal balance, for analogous reasons the extent to which a country's fiscal balance is moved in the direction of surplus (or deficit) is no sort of guide to whether a given change in fiscal policy will be tending to improve or worsen the country's balance on current account. For some combinations of fiscal measures tending to reduce the fiscal deficit (or to move it into surplus) will tend to worsen the current account balance; whereas others (having the same effect on the fiscal balance), will tend to improve it. This general conclusion is always valid provided that different fiscal measures have different effects on the current account deficit for a given effect on the fiscal balance. As that seems certain to be true of some or all fiscal measures, it is not a conclusion that rests merely on particular empirical results such as those discussed above.

The most general conclusion ought therefore be that we must stop trying to assess the extent of the effects of different macroeconomic policies – whether on output, prices or the state of the current account – by looking at their effects on fiscal balances. The only analysis that is likely to be helpful is one that relates changes in particular fiscal instruments to their respective effects on all the macroeconomic objectives that are of interest – real output or employment; 'inflation' (as indicated by the upward pressure on prices over the period that is of interest to the policy maker); and the state of a country's current account plus or minus any change in the level of useful productive investment. If rational policies are to be devised and implemented a framework of analysis that involves these three broad macroeconomic objectives and at least three instruments (more if different types of taxes are also included) must always be employed in appraising policy and prescribing appropriate measures to meet any given situation.

7 Three Instruments and Three Objectives: A Framework for Analysis

This chapter extends and builds upon the analysis in Chapter 4 relating to the use of two or more macroeconomic instruments to influence two macroeconomic objectives. But the extension of the analysis to include three macroeconomic objectives greatly extends the number of logically possible assumptions about the possible combinations of effects (their direction, and whether they are negligible) of each of the instruments upon each objective. For we now have to take account of the possibility that each of *three* instruments will affect each of the *three* objectives in an upward or a downward direction, or that the effect of an instrument on an objective may be negligible; also to take account of the fact that the direction in which any given instrument should be changed may depend upon the relative extent of the effect of each of the three instruments on each objective if appropriate policies are to be adopted to bring the state of the economy closer to the government's macroeconomic objectives.

In theory, if we knew the exact effect of each instrument on each objective we could proceed to set each of them at the desired level to achieve all the macroeconomic objectives – provided only that each of them has a different relative effect on each objective. But in practice no government knows enough about the precise size of these effects to move straight to that point. Macroeconomic policy making has therefore always to be by way of a process of trial and error, making use of the best available evidence about the effects of each instrument on each of the objectives.

The analysis in the present chapter of the relative effects of each of the available instruments on each of the macroeconomic objectives therefore assumes only that the government has either a sufficient *a priori* presumption, or empirical evidence (or both), such as that outlined in the two preceding chapters, about the direction and the relative size of each of these effects to guide it in selecting the appropriate *directions* in which to change its available instruments in order to bring the economy closer to the desired macroeconomic objectives. At the very least, the information available, if considered in the sort of framework suggested in this chapter, should make it possible to avoid changing the instruments in directions that can be expected (on the available evidence) to drive the economy (further) away from the desired macroeconomic situation.

Examples will be given of changes that will tend to raise output, reduce prices and improve the current account (or increase thrift). (Clearly other combinations of aims about the directions in which the macroeconomy should be changed would require appropriate modifications to the analysis.) There will in any given case be a number of combinations of changes that will move the economy in the desired directions; the examples will merely illustrate that such combinations of measures are possible. The choice *among* the possible combinations of changes that will operate in the desired directions will depend on the relative importance attached by the government to each of the macroeconomic objectives, and on how rapidly the government wishes to move towards each of them.

As all the figures in the illustrative prescriptions consist of ratios, the implication is that all the figures could be multiplied by some constant figure to give larger (or smaller) changes. Of course, in reality, one cannot be sure that the relative effects would continue to be the same if large changes were made: and one might hope that eventually governments would able to obtain enough evidence to estimate how far, if at all, the relative effect of each instrument on each objective would diminish or increase as greater use was made of an instrument in a particular direction. It should also be borne in mind that the extent and direction of effects may vary according to the time since the policy change was introduced; and that these lags may be different for the effects of different instruments on different objectives. The period over which a government wishes to work towards its objectives may therefore also be relevant to its choice of measures.

Another preliminary matter that should be emphasised here is that the approach outlined in this chapter assumes nothing about whether governments can and should vary policy settings with great frequency ('discretion') or only on the basis of certain broad guidelines ('rules of thumb'). This depends partly upon how promptly the government acts and on how quickly the economy responds to any changes in policy. The analysis that follows relates simply to the sort of effects that could be expected to ensue once the economy has reacted, and makes no assumption or assertion about how frequently a government should vary the setting of its policy instruments. For the same broad principles – relating to the direction and the relative extent to which each instrument should be changed – are relevant, whether or not a government changes its policy settings frequently.

In view of the large number of combinations of logically possible assumptions – very few of which could be ruled out completely as unlikely to be relevant for *some* economy in *some* historical period – the analysis has to be highly selective about the choice of particular combinations of assumptions that are chosen to illustrate the principles involved. If combinations of assumptions other than those discussed in the present chapter are believed to be relevant for a particular country at some particular time, however, it should be clear from the analysis of the present chapter how the application of the basic principles illustrated by the cases analysed would enable the government of a different sort of economy, where one of the other combinations of assumptions seemed more likely, to work towards the achievement of its macroeconomic objectives.

The selection of cases for analysis in this chapter has been based on two principles: in the first place, it covers those combinations of assumptions that seem most likely to be of practical relevance judging by the *a priori* analysis and the empirical evidence of previous chapters; and, in the second place, other hypothetically possible combinations of assumptions are chosen that may serve to illustrate the broad principles, selecting principally combinations of assumptions that do not depart very far from those that seem most likely (on the *a priori* arguments and empirical evidence of previous chapters) to be relevant to the real world.

The analysis is confined to three macroeconomic instruments. These are in most cases thought of as being monetary policy (using a cut in interest rates as the indicator of changes in this); government outlays; and tax cuts. In each case the instrument is defined in an 'expansionary' direction – that is, using it in the direction that would normally be expected to increase real output and employment. But, for some combinations of assumptions, it might be better to think of the three instruments as government outlays, cuts in indirect taxes (or in payroll taxes), and cuts in direct taxes. In any case, the analysis is to be taken as quite general. The three instruments could have been identified merely as 'instrument A, instrument B and instrument C'. But most people find it easier to follow an analysis that refers to a real macroeconomic instrument, so that in the illustrative examples the instruments will be identified as particular types of macroeconomic policy measure. It should be borne in mind, however, that the labels on each of the rows (illustrating the effects of a particular instrument on a particular objective) can be interchanged without loss of relevance. For instance, where an example assumes that monetary policy has no effect on one objective (say, real output), an appropriate change in the labels showing the names of instruments or in the position of the zero could also cover the case where a cut in taxes had no effect on prices. To avoid unnecessary repetition, therefore, only one combination of a given set of effects will be considered (without going through other permutations of the same sets of assumptions), as the same analysis would follow (with an appropriate change in the position of the figures in each table – the names of the instruments and the objectives) to cover cases where it is a different instrument and a different objective to which the assumed effect relates. For example, in the case mentioned above – a zero effect of one instrument on one of the objectives – the zero effect might be that of monetary policy on output or, alternatively, that of indirect tax cuts on prices.

In illustrating the sets of assumptions and the policy prescriptions that follow from them (and as an extension of the procedure followed for the examples in Chapter 4) the convention is adopted of showing in the first column – that showing the effect on real output (or employment) – a series of figure '1's. This is because we want to see the relative effect of each instrument on each of the other two objectives *for a given effect on one of the objectives* – which we shall consistently take to be its effect on real output – which may be thought of as an upward effect equal to one per cent of real GDP over the relevant period (but which could alternatively be interpreted as a rise of 1 per cent in employment). (The figures could, of course, have been standardised in the same way in terms of the effects of each of them on one of the other objectives.)

The figures in the second and third columns are thus to be interpreted simply as ratios showing the relative effects of each instrument on that objective when they are being changed on a sufficient scale to have the stated effect on the objective in column 1. The units used in one column are therefore not comparable with those used in another. For example, the effect on prices would be in terms of a percentage change in the price level over the average of years covered by the case under consideration, whereas that on output is in terms of a given percentage change in the level of real GDP over the same period.

If an instrument had no effect on real output, the relative effect of that instrument would have to be standardised in terms of its effect on one of the other objectives. In such cases, we are therefore comparing the relative effects of all three instruments on only two of the objectives, and the ratios of only two of them on the objective that is unaffected by the third instrument. If an instrument has no effect on two objectives (as may be true of the effect of monetary measures on employment and on the current account, for some countries, and over some periods) the figure shown in the column for the objective that it affects is completely arbitrary – only the sign being relevant to the analysis. But the extent of the change of monetary policy required to have the stated effect on prices (for the stated changes in the other instruments) is an important element in the prescription derived from such a set of assumptions.

METHOD OF THE ANALYSIS

The macroeconomic objectives chosen to illustrate these examples will always include the letter 'O' as the heading for the first column – to indicate 'real *o*utput' (though it could also be interpreted as 'employment'); and 'P' for '*p*rices'. The third column will sometimes be headed 'T' for '*t*hrift' – signifying the effect on private investment less any rise in the current account deficit (or plus any movement in the direction of current account surplus); but it will sometimes (where the assumptions being made in the example are more appropriately related to the narrower objective) be headed 'C' for 'the *c*urrent account balance' (a negative sign indicating that the effect will be to move that balance in the direction of a larger deficit).

To avoid any confusion between the target, 'thrift', and the instrument, 'tax cuts', the target will always be referred to as 'T' and the instrument as 'TC'. If that instrument is moved negatively, therefore, that will represent a *rise* in tax rates. Both of the fiscal instruments are defined in the context of a constant monetary policy (taken as holding the quantity of money constant, rather than holding interest rates constant). The instruments are defined as operating in an expansionary direction – thus limiting the cases to those (presumably, generally the only realistic ones) where a tax cut or a rise in government spending does not actually lead to a fall in real output or employment. If there are circumstances where a tax cut would reduce real output (or even have a zero net effect on it) there could clearly be no upward effect on prices resulting from any stimulus to demand (as there would in that case be none), so that the tax cuts could then only reduce costs and prices. A cut in tax rates would in that case be an instrument that could only have a helpful effect in checking inflation, but could not be used to raise real output or employment. (G = government outlays).

SOME STRAIGHTFORWARD CASES

As in Chapter 4, there are some straightforward (if highly unlikely) cases where the policy conclusions are evident. There is first the case – which is by implication that which appears to be assumed in the standard literature and in many policy decisions (but for which we have found no support on *a priori* grounds or in the empirical evidence) – that each instrument has the same relative effect (which may be zero in some cases) on all three objectives. Just as in a simple international trade model (with identical tastes in all countries) there would be no trade if no country had a comparative advantage in the production of any commodity, in the same way there would be no possibility of varying the mix of different instruments in such a way as to work towards all three objectives if the ratios of the effects of each of them on each of the objectives were the same. In effect, the available instruments would not then be independent of one another, and could not be used as if they were. It would therefore be equivalent to having only one macroeconomic instrument.

It is intuitively even less likely that this situation could ever arise when there are three (or more) instruments available that may be changed independently than if there are only two. But in cases where there may be no comparative advantage between *two* of the instruments in dealing with *two* of the objectives, the effects of the third instrument together with differences in the relative effects of each of the first two instruments on the third objective, may still make it possible to move the economy towards all of its objectives.

A very different set of assumptions to that which assumes there is no comparative advantage among the instruments – but also carrying the implication that there would under those assumptions be no policy available to move the economy towards all three of its objectives – would be the obvious case where none of the three instruments has any effect on any of the three objectives; for in that case obviously nothing can be done to solve the problems. There may also (more realistically) be cases where one or more of the objectives is not affected by any of the three instruments; but where it may still be possible to move the economy closer to the other two objectives; and as that could not then have an adverse effect on the third objective, that would certainly constitute an improvement.

Similarly, if there is even one instrument that can improve the situation in terms of one of the objectives without having an adverse effect on either of the other objectives, an appropriate change in the setting of that instrument will improve the situation, even if the other instruments have no effect on any of the objectives. Or if two of the objectives can be favourably affected without an adverse effect on the third, it is obviously possible to improve the situation, though not necessarily to move closer to more than two of the objectives.

We shall consider first those cases that appear to be the most realistic, on the basis of the arguments and evidence outlined in earlier chapters. But the figures chosen will be simplified, generally taking the smallest whole numbers that illustrate the principles involved, without attempting to reproduce the exact ratios implied in any of the empirical evidence for the effects of different instruments on an objective. It is important, however, to choose figures that reproduce the essence of the relative extent of any comparative advantage for one instrument over another in dealing with two or more objectives (so far as the empirical evidence helps us to assess this); and the ratios chosen will therefore parallel so far as possible the ranking of the ratios that would imply the policy conclusions that can be drawn from the evidence cited in Chapters 3 and 6.

TWO INSTRUMENTS AND THREE OBJECTIVES

Let us consider first some cases where two instruments taken alone will suffice to bring the economy closer to three objectives.

Table 7.1 (like the others in this chapter) is to be interpreted as showing, on the left-hand side, the assumptions about the relative effects of each instrument on each of the objectives if each instrument is changed sufficiently to raise real GDP by one percentage point over the period towards which policy is being directed. On the right-hand side are shown the ratios of the effects on the various objectives of selected combinations of changes in the instruments that would (on the basis of those assumptions) move each of the objectives in the desired direction.

Table 7.1 shows a case where the use of only two policy instruments can bring the economy closer to all three macroeconomic objectives (assuming that these aims are to raise real output, reduce the upward

Table 7.1 Two fiscal instruments to promote three objectives

	Assumptions			*Prescriptions*		
	O	P	C	O	P	C
G	+1	+2	−2	−1	−2	+2
TC	+1	+1	−1	+1.1	+1.1	−1.1
Net effect				+0.1	−0.9	+0.9
or						
G				−1	−2	+2
TC				+1.9	+1.9	−1.9
Net effect				+0.9	−0.1	+0.1

pressure on prices and improve the current account balance). This is because (as is consistent with the balance of the arguments and the evidence adduced in earlier chapters) a cut in taxes has less (if any) upward effect on prices *and also* less upward effect on any current account deficit than does a rise in government outlays having the same effect on real output. Of course, if the government's aim were to reduce a current account *surplus*, it would not then be possible on the assumptions in the table to move towards all of its objectives simultaneously, as any combination of tax cuts and government outlays that provided a non-inflationary, or price-reducing, stimulus would tend to *increase* the current account surplus. In that case a third instrument would be required – on the lines of later examples in this chapter.

The corollary of this prescription is that, given the stated assumptions, a government that tries to provide a stimulus by raising government outlays, and to correct the resulting upward pressure on prices and on the current account deficit by increasing taxes, would tend to make matters worse on at least two fronts; and the consequent adverse effects on the combination of real output, prices and the state of the current account would drive the economy further away from the desired situation on some (or even on all) of these objectives, until the government replaced the mix of higher government outlays and higher taxes by one of lower outlays and lower taxes. (Similar policy conclusions about the types of mixes to *avoid* can be derived by reversing all the policy prescriptions in this chapter – as with those in Chapter 4.)

Another case where two instruments would be sufficient to work towards three objectives is where monetary policy has a greater superiority over one of the fiscal instruments in its effects on prices than in its effects on private investment (and so on thrift), for a given effect on real output or employment, but where both instruments affect all the objectives in the same direction. Table 7.2 gives an example of this.

In the case illustrated in Table 7.2, monetary policy is to be moved in the contractionary direction, in order to hold down prices, because it is on that objective that its relative effect is the greater. The adverse effect on thrift of such a change in monetary policy can be offset by a tax cut in this case, without fully offsetting the downward effect of the tightening of monetary policy upon prices, and while still giving a net stimulus to output.

If, however, the aim had been to *reduce* thrift while stimulating output and reducing the upward pressure on prices, the use of these two instruments alone would have been insufficient. For if tax cuts had been on a scale sufficient to reduce thrift in the face of a tightening of monetary policy sufficient to reduce prices, there would have been a net downward effect on output.

Moreover, even if the use of two instruments alone would be able to move the economy towards all three objectives, a government will have available to it a much larger range of options about the extent of the changes in the macroeconomic objectives that it can bring about if it can make use of three instruments, rather than merely two.

For example, on the assumptions shown in Table 7.2 about monetary policy, and also the same assumptions as in those in Table 7.1 about the fiscal instruments, a much greater downward pressure could be exerted on prices by a combination of measures leading to a similar improvement in the current account balance for the same (marginal) rise in real output (as Table 7.3 shows). As monetary policy does not in this case have a significant effect on the current account balance, the policy of trying to use a tightening of monetary policy to improve the

Table 7.2 Use of tax cuts and monetary policy to promote three objectives

	Assumptions			*Prescriptions*		
	O	P	T	O	P	T
Cut in r	+1	+7	+3	−1.0	−7.0	−3.0
TC	+1	+2	+1	+3.1	+6.2	+3.1
Net effect				+2.1	−0.8	+0.1

r = rate of interest

Table 7.3 Use of three instruments to promote three objectives

	Assumptions			*Policy prescriptions*		
	O	P	C	O	P	C
Cut in r	+1	+3	0	−1	−3	0
G	+1	+2	−2	−2	−4	+4
TC	+1	+1	−1	+3.1	+3.1	−3.1
Net effect				+0.1	−3.9	+0.9
				or		
				−1	−3	0
				−2	−4	+4
				+3.9	+3.9	−3.9
Net effect				+0.9	−3.1	+0.1
				or		
				−1	−3	0
				−2.5	−5	+5
				+4.9	+4.9	−4.9
Net effect				+1.4	−3.1	+0.1

current account could not work towards that objective, though it would exert a useful downward pressure on prices. The latter effect would mean, however, that a greater reduction in tax rates (and so a greater stimulus to real output) would be consistent with a given net downward effect on prices than if only the two fiscal instruments had been available. Alternatively, a greater upward effect on output, and a greater downward pressure on prices for a given favourable effect on the current account, is possible with these three instruments, as Table 7.3 also shows.

There are several types of cases (other than that where neither instrument affects one or more objectives) where changes in combinations of the two fiscal instruments will not be able to give a non-inflationary real stimulus while improving the current account.

One of these is if the relative effects of a rise in government outlays on prices, compared with that of a tax cut having the same effect on real output or employment, are the same as their relative effects on the current account. In this case, any cut in government outlays sufficient to exert downward pressure on prices in the face of a tax cut sufficient to provide a net stimulus to output will worsen the current account (see Table 7.4).

Another case where the two fiscal instruments alone cannot be varied in such a way as to give a non-inflationary stimulus without worsening

Table 7.4 Two instruments and three objectives: an inappropriate assignment

	Assumptions			*Example of policy failure*		
	O	P	C	O	P	C
Rise in G	+1	+2	+2	−0.55	−1.1	−1.1
TC	+1	+1	+1	+1.0	+1.0	+1.0
Net effect				+0.45	−0.1	−0.1

the current account is if government outlays have the greater upward effect on prices (for a given real stimulus) and tax cuts have a greater effect in the direction of worsening the current account (or where those two effects are exactly offsetting). (See Tables 7.5 and 7.6).

In this case, any reduction of government outlays sufficient to exert downward pressure on prices in the face of a tax cut that will leave a net stimulus will improve the current account by less than the rise in the current account deficit that will result from a tax cut that will provide a net real stimulus.

In either of these cases (comparative advantages that operate in opposite directions, and in the ratios shown, on prices and thrift respectively, or comparative advantages of the two fiscal instruments that are the same on both prices and thrift) a third instrument would be required to provide a net inflationary stimulus that would also improve the current account (or thrift – if that is the third objective).

Let us take the third instrument to be monetary policy, and take first the case where its comparative advantage over both the fiscal instruments in stimulating thrift exceeds its comparative advantage in affecting prices (for a given real stimulus).

If the ratios of the effects of the two fiscal instruments on prices are the same as those of their respective effects on thrift (for a given real

Table 7.5 Two instruments and three objectives: an inappropriate assignment

	Assumptions			*Example of policy failure*		
	O	P	T	O	P	T
Reduction in government outlays	+1	+2	−1	−0.55	−1.1	+0.55
TC	+1	+1	−2	+0.6	+0.6	−1.2
Net effect				+0.05	−0.5	−0.65

Table 7.6 Two instruments and three objectives: a further example of an inappropriate assignment

	Assumptions			*Example of policy failure*		
	O	P	C	O	P	C
Reduction in government outlays	+1	+3	−1	−1	−3	+1
TC	+1	+1	−2	+1.1	+1.1	−2.2
Net effect				+0.1	−1.9	−1.2

stimulus), so that changes in them alone cannot be used to reduce prices and increase thrift, it will be appropriate to use monetary policy with an eye to its effects on thrift – in which its advantage over the two fiscal instruments is greater than that which it has in dealing with prices. It will then be appropriate to use the two fiscal instruments to deal with the other two objectives – reducing government outlays to exert downward pressure on prices (for reasons already analysed with two instruments) and using tax cuts to stimulate output.

Taking the same assumptions about the fiscal instruments, but now assuming that monetary policy has a relatively smaller comparative advantage in dealing with prices than with thrift, however, it would be appropriate to use monetary policy in an expansionary direction (indicated by a cut in the rate of interest) to exert an upward effect on thrift (as illustrated in Table 7.8).

As Tables 7.7 and 7.8 show, an expansionary change in monetary policy may be combined with a tax cut and a cut in government outlays to give an upward effect on thrift and downward effect on prices.

Table 7.7 Three instruments and three objectives: an appropriate assignment

	Assumptions			*Prescriptions*		
	O	P	T	O	P	T
G	+1	+2	+2	−3	−6	−6
TC	+1	+1	+1	+2.9	+2.9	+2.9
Cut in r	+1	+3	+4	+1	+3	+4
Net effect				+0.1	−0.1	+0.9

r = rate of interest

Table 7.8 Three instruments and three objectives: further examples of appropriate assignments

	Assumptions			*Prescriptions*		
	O	P	T	O	P	T
G	+1	+3	−1	−2.2	−6.6	−2.2
TC	+1	+1	−2	+1.3	+1.3	−2.6
Cut in r	+1	+4	+5	+1.0	+4.0	+5.0
Net effect				+0.1	−1.3	+0.2
					or	
G	1	3	−1	−1.1	−3.3	+1.1
TC	1	1	−2	+0.2	+0.2	−0.4
Cut in r	1	2	5	+1.0	+2.0	+5.0
Net effect				+0.1	−1.1	+5.7

r = rate of interest

CONCLUSIONS

With three instruments and three objectives there are many thousands of logically possible combinations of assumptions about the direction of the effects of each instrument on each objective, and whether it has a negligible effect. There are also many different sets of assumptions about the ranking of the ratios of the effects of the three instruments on any one objective. Any of these combinations of assumptions is likely to give a different set of policy prescriptions, and it is difficult to rule out *a priori* the possibility that any of them might be relevant for some country at some time.

But one could probably rule out as highly unlikely (for reasons discussed in the closed economy context in Chapter 4) the possibility of an easing of monetary policy leading to downward pressure on prices – at any rate, if it did not simultaneously give a strong stimulus to real output. It also seems highly unlikely that an easing of monetary policy would actually reduce thrift, or that monetary expansion would have a greater adverse effect (if any) on the current account balance than any form of fiscal stimulus. But, for the reasons already discussed in the closed economy context, either form of fiscal stimulus, with a constant quantity of money, could either raise or reduce real output (though the possibility of tax cuts reducing real output seems very slight); and either form of fiscal expansion could exert either an upward or a downward pressure on prices; or, of course, have a negligible effect on real output or prices. Either fiscal measure might, in principle, have either an upward or a downward, or a negligible, effect on thrift; but it seems highly unlikely that either form of fiscal stimulus, with a constant quantity of money, could actually improve the current account balance.

The combinations of assumptions chosen for the illustrations in this chapter have been mainly ones that appear to be most likely to be relevant – in the light of the *a priori* arguments given in Chapter 5 and the empirical evidence in Chapter 6.

The first examples in this chapter illustrated asumptions on which changes in only two instruments can suffice to bring the economy closer to all three objectives (real output or employment, inflation, and thrift or the state of the current account). If the aim is to provide a non-inflationary, or price-reducing, stimulus without reducing thrift (or, with the alternative third objective, without worsening the current account balance), changes in the two fiscal instruments can be used for this purpose if the one that has less upward effect on prices for a given real stimulus is also that which has less adverse effect on thrift (or on the current account). The *a priori* arguments of Chapter 5 and the empirical evidence of Chapter 6 suggested that this is the typical case. If the fiscal measure that had the greater upward effect on prices for a given real stimulus had also a greater adverse effect on the current account, it would also be possible, by moving that instrument in a contractionary direction and with an appropriate stimulus being provided by the other, to provide a price-reducing stimulus that would tend to reduce an external deficit and reduce prices. If the more inflationary instrument had the less adverse effect on the current account, however, a similar combination of measures could reduce inflation and reduce a current account *surplus*.

For countries concerned to hold down the current account deficit, as well as for those that wish to reduce a current account surplus, changes within the fiscal mix may thus often be sufficient to improve the macroeconomic situation on all three objectives, with one of the sorts of changes of mix – reductions in government outlays and taxes – that we saw to be appropriate in the closed economy for providing a non-inflationary stimulus.

But the other type of mix that was appropriate in the closed economy for providing a non-inflationary stimulus – a tight monetary policy and tax cuts or increases in government outlays – is less likely to be helpful for providing a price-reducing stimulus while improving the current account in the open economy, as the tightening of monetary policy, which operates to exert downward pressure on prices, is likely to have little or no effect (and of an uncertain direction) on the current account balance. It will, moreover, tend to reduce thrift, and a fiscal expansion is likely to reduce thrift, or, at best, if it increases thrift – as some types of tax cuts might do – be likely to do so by considerably less than the downward effect on thrift resulting from a monetary contraction that reduces prices in the face of the expansionary fiscal measure.

If, however, the tax cut is of the type that exerts downward pressure on prices while providing a real stimulus, the use of a monetary *expansion* to increase thrift may be consistent with the provision of a price-reducing stimulus and a rise in thrift. If the aim were to reduce a current account deficit, however, in the face of the worsening in it that would result from the tax cut, it is highly unlikely that a tightening of monetary policy would contribute to that end.

Three instruments will often be needed in order to work towards all three objectives. Moreover, with three instruments, a wider range of different quantitative outcomes is almost always possible – even if the use of two instruments alone would have had some effect in the desired directions on all objectives.

But three instruments will be necessary if the ratios of the effects of two of the instruments – say, the two fiscal instruments – on each of two of the objectives are the same. If the third instrument – say, monetary policy – has a different effect on one of those objectives for a given effect on the other, and if the two fiscal instruments have different effects on the third objective (for given effects on the other two), the use of the third instrument will be necessary, and will in that case make it possible to work towards all three objectives.

Moreover, the third instrument will also be required if one of the fiscal instruments has a comparative advantage in dealing with prices, for example, whereas the other has the advantage in changing the current account in the desired direction.

The only cases where the use of three instruments is unlikely to be able to move the economy towards all three objectives will be if there are one or more objectives that cannot be affected by an instrument; or if the three instruments lack any comparative advantage in dealing with two, or even all three, of the objectives (that is, the ratios of their respective effects are the same on two, or on all three, of the objectives).

We have not found any case in the empirical evidence where one or more of the objectives was not affected by *any* of the instruments tested – limited though the range of those instruments was to certain types of tax and to government outlays *as a whole*; nor did the evidence suggest that there are cases where there is an absence of any comparative advantage among the instruments in dealing with two or three objectives. Indeed, *a priori* reasoning suggests that such cases where there is no comparative advantage are unlikely to occur.

The conclusion should be that the failure of governments to adopt combinations of measures that would enable them to work towards all three main macroeconomic objectives is not likely to be by reason of any inherent impossibility of working simultaneously towards all three aims. It is much more likely to be because of the widespread failure to enquire into, and to take account in macroeconomic policy making of, the relative effects of each of the available instruments on each of the macroeconomic objectives.

But though this seems to be a valid conclusion for individual countries, it is true that changes in the setting of monetary policy, on the one hand, together with simultaneous changes in one or more fiscal measures, on the other, operate to a large extent through the exchange rate (as we saw in Chapter 3). This may mean that an individual country using such a change of mix may often be solving its macroeconomic problems largely at the expense of other countries – though there is no presumption that a similar objection could be raised to the use of different combinations of changes in different *fiscal* measures in such a way as to work towards all three objectives.[1]

Consideration will therefore be given in Chapter 9 to the question of whether, if one is concerned with macroeconomic policy in the interests of the world as a whole, the policy prescriptions are likely to be different from those that are appropriate if one is concerned only for the immediate interests of an individual country.

NOTE

1. The objectives themselves may, of course, be incompatible between one country and another – especially if the majority of countries are all simultaneously trying to reduce their current account deficits. But this is not a defect of the use made of the available combinations of instruments, but arises from the macroeconomic objectives accepted by each government.

8 Deregulation and Macroeconomic Policy[1]

This chapter brings together a number of arguments that may be raised about the impact of various forms of financial deregulation on the efficacy of monetary policy for achieving the principal macroeconomic objectives, including its relative effectiveness as compared with fiscal policy. These considerations may thus have a bearing on the relative effects of monetary policy compared with fiscal instruments, and so on the choice of policy mixes. Even though some of these arguments are in principle fairly widely discussed and presumably widely accepted, there is reason to believe that, in some countries at least, their implications for the appropriate choice of macroeconomic measures (especially as to the best combinations of measures for reducing a current account deficit) have not been properly absorbed into the thinking of policy makers and their advisers.

Clearly, if the relative effect of different macroeconomic instruments has changed during the 1980s as a result of deregulation and the associated financial innovations, it may have affected the comparative advantages of the different instruments for achieving different objectives. Most of the arguments that we shall consider in this section relate primarily to the effects of the different instruments on nominal aggregate demand. For the most part, however, these arguments do not relate to any effects they may have upon the combination of real output and price increases associated with any given rise in (nominal) aggregate demand that results from any given expansionary measure.

They do, however, have implications for the extent of price rises associated with a given real stimulus so far as they have increased or reduced the extent of depreciation or appreciation of the currency that is associated with the rise in real output that results from any given form of stimulus; and, in this respect they therefore have implications for the relative effects on prices and output respectively of monetary measures, on the one hand, and fiscal measures (in general) on the other.

It is perhaps of particular importance to consider these matters here as much of the data on which the macroeconometric models used for the empirical evidence assembled in earlier chapters are based would have been derived from the period before the widespread financial deregulation of the 1980s – even though what was probably the most important form of deregulation, the move towards exchange rate flexibility, occurred in the early 1970s in the countries covered in these simulations. In other respects, however, we shall find that developments during the 1980s probably enhanced the differential effects on nominal aggregate demand and on the exchange rate of monetary policy, on the one hand, compared with fiscal measures, on the other; but that the general conclusion should be that the changes that have occurred during the 1980s are unlikely to have been such as to cast doubt on the *ranking* of the different macroeconomic instruments that is suggested by the empirical evidence and *a priori* arguments in this book, and in certain respects they are likely to have enhanced the comparative advantage of both types of fiscal measures over monetary policy for dealing with the current account.

THE DEREGULATION OF BANK DEPOSIT RATES

The process of deregulation has been accompanied and followed by – and has to a considerable extent brought about – a process of financial innovation leading to the payment of something closer to market rates of interest on many liquid assets that are either forms of money or near-money. To the extent that this is true, a rise (or fall) in nominal interest rates does not change the opportunity cost of holding money, so that there will not be as great a change in the demand for money (at a given level of aggregate demand) in response to a change in the general level of interest rates as used to occur when most forms of money were much less likely to bear something close to market rates of interest. This change to the payment of near-market rates of interest on many forms of near-money has much the same effect as a reduction in the responsiveness of the demand for money to changes in interest rates. But it is not appropriate to describe it as such, for the response of the demand for money to a *given* change in the opportunity cost of holding money may be the same as it was before the deregulation of interest rates. Nevertheless, it tends to make monetary policy more effective in influencing nominal aggregate demand, in much the same way as does a reduction in the responsiveness of the demand for money to a given change in interest rates.

This has certain implications for macroeconomic policy. Take first a closed economy, and compare the effects of a given tightening of monetary policy with those that would have ensued prior to deregulation of bank interest rates.

When monetary policy is tightened, the consequent rise in interest rates leads to some economising in the holding of cash balances (at any given level of nominal aggregate demand) – a rise in the velocity of circulation – and so to a weakening of the downward effect on aggregate demand. But the payment of something closer to market rates of interest on a number of types of money or near-money means that when monetary policy is tightened the opportunity cost of holding money does not rise as much as it did before the deregulation of bank deposit rates. This consideration means that a given tightening of monetary policy (measured as a given rise in the general level of interest rates resulting from monetary tightening) exerts, *ceteris paribus* a greater downward effect on aggregate demand than it did before deregulation (as the velocity of circulation does not tend to rise so much as it did when monetary policy was tightened in the past).

Now let us apply a similar analysis to the effects of a tightening of fiscal policy (assuming that it does not make any difference from this point of view whether this occurs by way of a rise in taxes or a fall in government outlays).

The effect of a tightening of fiscal policy, with a given quantity of money, is to reduce the demand for money (so far as it depends on aggregate demand), and so to reduce the general level of interest rates. Before deregulation, when the opportunity cost of holding money was thus reduced, the effect was to lead people to hold *more* money at a given level of activity than they would have done when interest rates were higher (because the incentive for economising in the holding of cash balances had been reduced). The velocity of circulation therefore fell, and that exerted a further downward pressure on aggregate demand – thus *reinforcing* the downward effect on activity of the tightening of fiscal policy, whereas the corresponding effect when monetary policy was tightened was (as we saw above) to *diminish* the effect of the change in monetary policy.

Post-deregulation, with something closer to market rates of interest now payable on many forms of 'money', however, when market interest rates fall this effect (an increase in the demand for cash balances at a given level of aggregate demand) will not occur to the same extent as in the past. That means that the payment of market rates of interest on many forms of money reduces the incentive for people to hold more money when interest rates fall as a result of a fiscal tightening; and this consideration (weakening the tendency for the velocity of circulation to fall) tends to make a tightening of fiscal policy *less* effective in reducing aggregate demand *than it was prior to the deregulation of interest rates* – especially relative to monetary policy.

One may hazard the guess that these considerations may have led central banks and governments around the world during the period since deregulation to be unduly confident about the extent to which monetary policy can influence aggregate demand (and perhaps also to underestimate the effectiveness of fiscal policy).

On the other hand, in the years during and following financial deregulation, monetary authorities have probably become readier to allow interest rates to rise or fall. That would mean that – as it is still true that the opportunity cost of holding money changes to some extent with an easing or tightening of monetary policy – this would be an offsetting consideration providing *more* incentive for people to change their demand for money as monetary policy is eased or tightened. That would tend to work in the opposite direction to the effects discussed in the preceding paragraphs (which related to responses to a *given* change in the general level of interest rates).

OPEN ECONOMY ASPECTS

Let us now consider some aspects of these considerations that relate to the open economy.

We have seen above that a tightening of monetary policy now leads to the rates of interest paid on near-money rising by more than they did before deregulation. This means that there is now less incentive than there used to be for rising interest rates to lead to greater economy in the holding of cash balances. This intensifies the excess demand for money over its supply, and so increases the demand for extra capital inflow from overseas. This extra capital inflow leads to greater upward pressure on the value of the currency in the face of a tightening of monetary policy than would have occurred before deregulation.

Moreover, the deregulation of capital flows and other factors relating to the international integration of capital markets now make capital flows more responsive to interest rate differentials than they were in earlier years. The upshot is therefore that a given tightening of monetary policy (in terms of its direct effects on domestic demand) now has a greater upward effect on capital inflow, and to that extent on the value of the currency in foreign exchange markets, than it did before deregulation. Indeed, it may be argued that capital flows are now so mobile internationally that the main impact of monetary policy is on the exchange rate (through the consequent effects on capital flows), rather than on interest rates, at least in small and medium-sized economies.

Taken together, these effects tend to increase the power of a tightening of monetary policy to hold down price increases, by causing a greater appreciation of the currency than would have occurred in the past.

But this also means that a given tightening of monetary policy is less likely to have a favourable effect on the current account than it was before deregulation – and, indeed, more likely to have an *unfavourable* effect on it. For the greater appreciation of the currency that now occurs when monetary policy is tightened makes it likely that the consequent appreciation of the currency will offset (or even reverse) the favourable effect on the current account that would otherwise result from the fall in aggregate demand as monetary policy is tightened. Indeed, as a tightening of monetary policy tends to increase net capital inflow (at any given level of activity), it must to that extent, with a freely floating exchange rate, tend also to move the current account in the direction of a larger deficit (or smaller surplus). The general presumption ought therefore to be that a tightening of monetary policy may well now actually have an *adverse* effect on the current account, even in the short run; and in the medium run – when interest remittances to other countries rise as a result of the additional capital inflow – it becomes even more likely that the current account deficit will increase.

Indeed, if capital flows are so responsive to small changes in one country's interest rates that a country cannot increase its interest rates greatly relative to the rest of the world (except so far as people expect its currency to depreciate), the whole of the impact of a tightening of monetary policy in restraining demand has to operate through the exchange rate. It does this by discouraging exports and encouraging imports; so that its downward effect on domestic activity can come about *only* by way of a *deterioration* in the current account.

Are there any channels through which a tightening of monetary policy might, nevertheless, reduce a current account deficit?

One way in which that might occur would be if the tightening of monetary policy brought about a large fall in aggregate demand, *and if* the inflow of capital were appreciably more sensitive to the level of aggregate demand than to relative interest rates (as indicated by a tightening of monetary policy relative to that of the rest of the world). If this were to be a persuasive argument for the view that a tightening of monetary policy could improve the current account, however, one would require very convincing evidence that the fall in aggregate demand resulting from the tightening of monetary policy will have such a large downward effect on capital inflow as to exceed the upward effect on it through interest rate differentials that one would otherwise expect to result from the tighter monetary measures. *A priori* it seems very difficult to believe that a tightening of monetary policy will tend to reduce net capital inflow (that is, to improve the current acocount) – even after allowing for its effect by way of reducing aggregate demand.

But even if a tightening of monetary policy could succeed in improving the current account balance through this route, it would do so only with a substantially greater reduction in output and employment than would a tightening of fiscal policy (because of their respective effects on the exchange rate being in opposite directions, whereas their effects on capital inflow by way of their impact on aggregate demand would be the same). This was true even before deregulation, and is likely to be true *a fortiori* since deregulation and with the increasing international integration of capital markets.[2]

There may be other channels through which a tightening of monetary policy could improve the current account. A rise in interest rates could perhaps increase the propensity to save (at any given level of income or output) by more than a fiscal tightening (which tends to reduce interest rates). But the direction and extent of the effect of changes in interest rates upon the propensity to save seems uncertain, and is thus a dangerous reed on which to lean for this conclusion. In any case, with highly mobile capital flows, the main effect of tighter monetary policy is now on the exchange rate, rather than on the level of domestic interest rates.

For countries for which investment goods have a high import content it is possible that there might be a large change in the structure of demand resulting from a tightening of monetary policy that would reduce the demand for imports considerably at any given level of activity, and to that extent bring about an improvement in the current account. This could happen if a rise in interest rates led to a curtailment of investment demand and with it a very sharp fall in imports. But if the government is concerned (as it should be) to maintain the level of 'thrift' (real investment *less* the current account deficit) – the combined total of which is a more defensible objective for policy than the state of the current account taken by itself – this would surely not normally be an acceptable route for achieving an improvement in the current account. Indeed, no government should seek to improve the country's net external financial position at the cost of a fully offsetting reduction in its domestic wealth in the form of useful productive investment.

In general, the considerations discussed above imply that the presumptions raised in earlier chapters to the effect that a tightening of monetary policy is likely to have little effect (if any) in the direction of improving the current account has presumably been reinforced by the effects of the various forms of financial deregulation, and the associated financial innovations, considered above. As the effectiveness of monetary policy for influencing the exchange rate has presumably been enhanced, it is likely that its relative effect on prices (compared with real output) is therefore relatively greater (compared with that of fiscal measures) than before deregulation. But in other respects the relative effects of changes in monetary policy on prices for a given effect on real output (compared with those of fiscal measures) do not appear to have been clearly affected in either direction by the consequences of these forms of deregulation and associated forms of financial innovation, irrespective of their net effect on the ability of monetary policy to influence *nominal* aggregate demand.

DEREGULATION AND FISCAL POLICY IN THE OPEN ECONOMY

In an open economy, the downward effect on aggregate demand of a tightening of fiscal policy, which tends to reduce interest rates, consequently tends to bring about a fall in net capital inflow (at any given level of activity). Before deregulation of bank deposit rates, that effect was to some extent alleviated by the increased demand for cash balances (at any given level of activity) that resulted from the consequent appreciable fall in the opportunity cost of holding money, and that tended to prevent interest rates from falling as much as they would otherwise have done.

But with the widespread payment of near-market rates on many forms of money or near-money, that effect (a fall in the velocity of circulation when interest rates are reduced) is now much smaller than it was. This means that a tightening of fiscal policy will lead to bigger falls in interest rates than would have been true before deregulation; and the downward effects on capital inflow of a given fiscal tightening (for a given reduction in aggregate demand) will consequently be greater.

A given tightening of fiscal policy will therefore now lead to less appreciation (as interest rates will fall by more) than it would have done before the deregulation of bank deposit rates, and therefore to a greater improvement in the current account at any given level of activity. This means that, if a government wants to effect as big an improvement as possible in the state of the current account with a minimum downward effect on real output or employment, fiscal measures will be more useful for this purpose than they were before deregulation (at least so far as the opportunity cost of holding money has a bearing on the outcome).

In other words, the effects of the deregulation and financial innovations discussed above tend to reinforce the relative effectiveness of fiscal measures (compared with monetary measures) for influencing the state of the current account, for any given change in real output or employment. Moreover, as a given tightening of fiscal policy will now (on the basis of the arguments outlined above) lead to less appreciation (or a greater likelihood of depreciation) than before, this raises a presumption that a tightening of fiscal policy will have a smaller downward effect on prices (for a given effect on real output) than before; whereas a tightening of monetary policy (being now more likely than before to attract additional capital inflow) will be more likely than in the past to reduce price increases (especially as compared with fiscal measures) as a result of the process of deregulation and the accompanying financial innovations during the 1980s.

In short, the comparative advantage of monetary measures for holding down prices in the domestic economy and the relative advantage of (both sorts of) fiscal measures for dealing with the state of the current account have probably been enhanced by the types of financial deregulation considered above.

OTHER CONSIDERATIONS RELATING TO THE CLOSED ECONOMY

In assessing whether monetary policy has been made more effective or less effective in influencing nominal aggregate demand by deregulation and by the various simultaneous forms of financial innovation, there are some other considerations that need to be set against the effect on the demand for money balances of the payment of something closer to market rates of interest on many forms of money or near-money.

In the first place, private expenditure may have become less sensitive to a given rise in market rates of interest – and this would tend to *reduce* the impact of monetary policy on aggregate demand (whereas the payment of interest on money tends, as we have seen, to *enhance* its effect on aggregate demand).

One general reason for this is that people now believe (with some justification) that they will always be able to obtain the funds they require – at some interest rate or other – now that rationing of credit is no longer an important channel for the operation of monetary policy.

It may well be that this consideration makes it more important to ensure that the government makes clear its intentions when it tightens monetary policy – and that if it wants a given rise in interest rates to have an appreciable effect in restraining demand it should not give the impression that it expects that interest rates will soon come down again.[3] This is not to say that there is any special connection between these announcement effects *as such* and the fact that monetary tightness now operates to a greater extent through the price mechanism and less by way of credit rationing (so that borrowers can nowadays usually rely on being able to obtain credit at some price or other). But if the process of deregulation has weakened the immediate impact of monetary tightening it becomes doubly important to ensure that the intentions of the authorities are made clear to the markets. Moroever, this also means that the government can ill afford to see the effect of a tightening of monetary policy weakened still further by giving the impression that it expects interest rates to come down again very shortly.

These considerations are reinforced by the fact that many loan contracts are nowadays on a floating interest rate basis.[4] This means that when an investor is considering whether to borrow in order to finance an outlay (on a house, or a factory, for example), it is less likely that a temporary rise in interest rates will now discourage the expenditure in question. For the borrower now knows that if market rates fall during the life of the loan, the rates on the loan will be reduced accordingly; whereas in the past it was usual for a borrower to be locked in for the full period of the loan to the rate of interest prevailing when the loan was arranged – and that was obviously a stronger incentive for a borrower to postpone the borrowing, and so the expenditure that it was to finance, when interest rates were felt to be temporarily high. The widespread use of floating rate loans may thus, on this view, have reduced the sensitivity of expenditure to changes in interest rates. It also means that a government is less likely than it would have been in the past to be able to achieve a temporary curtailment of investment spending by conveying the impression that interest rates are only temporarily high.

It may be argued, on the other hand, that the widespread adoption of floating rate loans may *enhance* the effectiveness of monetary policy. The argument is that, as a rise in interest rates now affects immediately not only those borrowers who are in the market this week, but also those who have borrowed in the past on a floating rate basis, this means that the *impact of a given tightening of monetary policy* is now much more widely spread over borrowers (whether they are in the market this week or not). That consideration has therefore to be set against those raised in the previous paragraph.

It is obviously an empirical matter which of the two considerations outlined in the two preceding paragraphs tends to dominate the other (or whether they neutralise one another). But one might express the *a priori* hunch that a rise in the interest rates paid this week by people who have borrowed in the past is not likely to have such a great impact on their expenditures – at least on capital investment in the immediate future – as will a change in the interest rates paid by firms or individuals who are borrowing this week to finance a particular outlay in the present or immediate future. (The latter, as has been argued above, are less likely to be discouraged, by what they perceive to be a temporary rise in market interest rates, from borrowing in order to invest than they would have been before the widespread use of floating rate loans.)

On balance, therefore, the much wider prevalence of floating rate loans seems likely to have made a tightening of monetary policy *less* effective (at least in the short run) in dampening investment spending. If that is true, it diminishes the force of the consideration that a tightening of monetary policy (with the aim of checking inflation) will have undesirable downward effects on private investment; and so enhances the comparative advantage of monetary policy for dealing with inflation (especially in view of the arguments relating to capital inflow and the exchange rate discussed above). It thus makes it more likely that a tightening of monetary policy (with the aim of checking inflation) will be an appropriate use of this instrument; and that the use of appropriate combinations of fiscal measures will be able to reverse any undesired downward effect on public and private investment resulting from the tightening of monetary policy.[5]

Another consideration is that mortgage contracts are nowadays much more likely to be such that the lender will merely extend the period of the loan, rather than increase the monthly payments, when market rates rise. There are also a number of other arrangements available whereby the immediate effect on the borrower of a rise in interest rates may be alleviated. In the short run, therefore, the borrower's expenditure is consequently less likely to be reduced by a given rise in market rates of interest (though in the longer run expenditure will presumably be reduced to more or less the same extent as it would have been under the old system).

It is also likely that increases in interest rates nowadays have a greater *upward* effect on the disposable incomes of households through the greater flexibility of the rates of interest paid on their bank (and other) deposits than was true before deregulation. It has even been suggested that in the US the immediate upward impact of higher interest rates on disposable incomes through the widespread payment of market rates of interest on near-money is likely to be more significant in its (upward) effects on household income and expenditure than the (downward) effect on their expenditure of any associated rises in mortgage rates – which take some time to flow through, depending on the lag before mortgage contracts are re-negotiated. In Australia, the continued existence of a number of mortgage borrowers whose rates are subject to a fixed ceiling would have something of the same effect – indeed, a more marked effect, though over only a minority of existing mortgage borrowers. The presumption should therefore be that the effects of a rise in interest rates on the disposable incomes of those households whose mortgages are subject to the interest rate ceiling would be upwards, if they own appreciable amounts of interest-bearing deposits. One could not reasonably suggest that this means that a rise in interest rates would actually raise total household disposable incomes in Australia, but it would be tending to weaken the downward effect of tighter monetary policy upon household incomes and expenditure.

There is therefore now a greater tendency for increases in interest rates to *raise* (some) disposable incomes and consumption expenditures than was true in the past – so that this effect should be set against whatever downward effect on spending may result from the rise in interest rates. This is especially likely to be true for lower income groups, who are on or below the lowest marginal income tax rates; for they are the income groups most likely to be among those benefitting by the payment of interest on current (checking) and savings accounts (in particular) rather closer to market rates than they were before deregulation. The proportion of any such rise in the disposable incomes of these income groups that is spent on additional consumption is likely to be especially high. This consideration, like those in the immediately preceding paragraphs, works in the direction of weakening the impact of monetary policy on aggregate demand.

The implications of the discussion of financial deregulation and innovation discussed in this chapter appear to be as follows.

On the one hand, the payment of market rates of interest on many forms of money tends to *enhance* the effectiveness of monetary policy. Nevertheless, it remains true that the total of non-interest bearing accounts is still large in many countries, even though they have not generally been rising nearly as fast as have interest-bearing accounts. Most countries are therefore probably not close to the extreme position (to which that in the US apparently approximates), where almost all forms of money (or almost all those forms of money the demand for which is likely to be responsive to changes in interest rates) bear market rates of interest.

On the other hand, a number of simultaneous changes (associated or at least coincident with deregulation) in the terms of many loan contracts, together with the upward effect on disposable incomes, especially those of lower income groups, of the payment of something closer to market rates of interest even on current and savings accounts, have presumably worked in the direction of *weakening* the impact on household incomes and expenditure of a given change in monetary policy.

If policy makers have been placing undue reliance on the first of these two effects (the one tending to enhance the effectiveness of monetary policy), they would therefore be inclined to have excessive confidence in the ability of a given tightening of monetary policy to restrain aggregate demand than would be warranted if *all* the various effects of deregulation (and of the associated financial innovations) had been given their due weight. For example, the progressive tightening of monetary policy that occurred over the course of 1988 and the first half of 1989 in both the UK and Australia seems to have had less effect in restraining demand than policy makers in those countries expected. But the analysis given above (relating to a number of factors that have probably tended to *weaken* the impact of monetary policy on nominal aggregate demand) implies that one should not be surprised that it was difficult to achieve the desired degree of restraint in aggregate demand by means of successive tightenings of monetary policy.

Exclusive (or disproportionate) emphasis in the minds of policy makers on those aspects of the introduction of floating-rate loans that may tend to enhance the effect of monetary policy, without due consideration of the factors outlined above that tend to weaken it (which may well be the dominant ones) would also be tending to make them unduly confident of the effectiveness of monetary policy for influencing effective demand.

At the same time, the consequent tendency for a given tightening of monetary policy (in terms of bond sales by the authorities) to place greater upward pressure on the general level of bank interest rates than before the deregulation of interest rates (leading to a sharper rise in capital inflow and a consequently greater appreciation of the currency), would, on this analysis, have tended to bring about a weakening of the current account at any given level of activity.

Especially if it is true that a tightening of monetary policy has come to have less effect in restraining domestic demand, and as it has become less likely to improve (and more likely to worsen) the current account at any given level of activity, by analogous reasoning the comparative advantage of fiscal measures for dealing with the current account will therefore have been enhanced. It is even possible that whereas in the past a tightening of monetary policy would have been more likely to reduce inflation without having a great upward effect on the exchange rate (and a consequent worsening of the current account at any given level of activity), it may now tend to weaken, rather than strengthen, the current account in the process of achieving a given reduction in the upward pressure on prices.

If it is true that when monetary policy is tightened the consequent appreciation is now likely to worsen the state of the current account at any given level of activity, whether or not this still leaves a net improvement in the current account it will mean that a greater sacrifice of output and employment would be required for any given improvement in the current account that might result than would the use of a fiscal measure of restraint.

This means that relatively more reliance needs to be placed on fiscal measures if one aim of policy is to improve the state of the current account (or the level of thrift, which includes the current account balance). For the efficacy of fiscal measures as a means of improving the current account with a minimum sacrifice of real output or employment, will have been enhanced by the deregulation of interest rates and by the much freer international flow of capital. This is because, as we saw above, a tightening of fiscal policy (leading to lower interest rates) will now be less likely to lead to a substantial rise in the holding of cash balances, and so less likely to have its downward effect on aggregate demand intensified by the holding of larger cash balances (at any given level of activity): while, at the same time, as interest rates on near-money are now much freer to rise and fall than they were prior to deregulation, and, as capital flows are now more responsive to relative interest rates than they used to be, this tends to reduce capital inflow by more (for a given tightening of fiscal policy) and thus to lead to a weaker exchange rate, and to that extent a stronger current account, at any given level of activity.

CONCLUSIONS

The implications of the financial deregulation of the 1980s for the ranking of the various policy measures discussed in earlier chapters appear to be as follows.

In the first place, the relative effects of monetary policy on prices for a given effect in restraining real output or employment has probably been enhanced by the increased influence of monetary measures on the exchange rate.

But, secondly, the usefulness of monetary policy for affecting the state of the current account has been reduced (by comparison with fiscal measures) by the same influences operating through the exchange rate.

In general, therefore, the ranking of measures (monetary versus both sorts of fiscal policy) that emerged from the discussion of earlier chapters seems likely to have been reinforced, so far as it operates through the exchange rate. We have found no prima facie justification for concluding that the process of financial deregulation, and the accompanying financial innovations, have appreciably weakened the arguments of earlier chapters to the effect that monetary policy is likely to be the most efficient instrument for affecting domestic price increases, but the least effective (because of its costs in terms of output and investment forgone) for improving the current account balance.

NOTES

1. I am indebted to Jerry Stein for very helpful discussions about a number of the matters raised in this chapter. I am of course alone responsible for remaining deficiencies. I have discussed several of these issues further in *The Deregulation of the Australian Financial System*, Melbourne University Press, 1989.
2. See Chapter 6, especially Table 6.1, for evidence that a tightening of monetary policy is likely to have less (if any) effect in the direction of improving the current account for any given effect on real output than are either of the fiscal measures tested.
3. David Chessell has suggested this to me.
4. This is presumably in part at least a consequence of the deregulation of interest rates; for an important reason why banks have become readier

to make floating rate loans is presumably that they are now able to raise interest rates on these contracts when market rates rise, whereas this might have been difficult or impossible when their lending rates were subject to a ceiling.

5. Malcolm Edey has suggested to me that the term structure of interest rates may well have adjusted to take account of the move towards floating rates of interest; so far as that is true the various effects outlined in the above paragraphs would presumably have been smaller, or even negligible.

9 The Macroeconomic Mix and the World Economy

The arguments and empirical evidence of earlier chapters have all been from the veiwpoint of an individual country (or, in the case of the simulations for the EEC as a whole, for a group of countries) in terms of the effects of alternative macroeconomic policies on the country adopting the policy. In this final chapter we set the analysis of the earlier chapters in the context of the world economy; asking whether there is reason to believe that an appropriate use of the macroeconomic policy instruments for solving the macroeconomic problems of individual countries will have adverse, or helpful, effects on the rest of the world, and on the world as a whole.

It is tempting to generalise from the prescription for one country to a prescription for the world as a whole. For it is true that if *all* countries are *successfully* maintaining high levels of employment and high rates of growth of real output with as little upward pressure on prices as possible, the world as a whole is likely to be able to avoid both serious unemployment and serious inflation. But some elements in the policies that are most likely to promote macroeconomic objectives for one country may make it harder for other countries to do the same.

In particular, we saw in Chapters 2 and 3 that part of the reason why a tight monetary policy can normally be expected to have a helpful effect in restraining the upward pressure on prices was because of its effects (over the short and medium term) in causing the currency of the country operating the tight monetary policy to appreciate. So far as that is true, it may reasonably be argued that the success of one country in holding down the upward pressure on prices would be at the expense of other countries, whose currencies would consequently have depreciated. It is possible, however, that the other countries might not have been so concerned to hold down inflation as was the country operating the tight monetary policy. Certainly, if the element of a tight monetary policy in an appropriate macroeconomic mix for checking both inflation and unemployment is used mainly by countries that are the most troubled by inflation, one could argue that – despite some upward pressure on the prices of other countries that might result from it –

there would presumably be an improvement in the world macroeconomic situation.

But, as the exchange rate is an important channel for this effect, it is certainly true that if all countries are relying on a mix with tight monetary policy as a means of trying to hold down inflation (at any given level of employment or economic growth) they will be less successful in achieving that aim for the world economy as a whole than an individual country (or group of countries, such as the EEC) would be if it operated that mix by itself.

Some of the *a priori* arguments in Chapter 2, did not, however, rely solely on the effects of tight monetary policy operating through the exchange rate to hold down price increases at any given level of employment or real output: and some of the empirical evidence in Chapter 3 was consistent with the view that there are also other channels through which a tight monetary policy may be expected to have a greater downward effect on prices for a given reduction in real output or employment than would tight fiscal measures (especially tax increases).

But, on balance, the effect of monetary tightness in holding down price increases through purely domestic channels (that is, excluding its effects operating through the exchange rate) are likely to be relatively small by comparison with its effects operating through the exchange rate. If, therefore, the problem for the world as a whole is to hold down inflation, one could feel less confident from a global viewpoint in prescribing a mix with tight monetary policy than one could for individual countries.

One could, however, reasonably advocate such a policy for those countries that are suffering from an appreciably higher rate of inflation than the rest of the world. But one should bear in mind that, so far as they are successful in operating it, a good deal of the success they may achieve is likely to be at the expense of greater upward pressure on prices in other countries. One would not, therefore, recommend mixes that included relatively tight monetary policies so strongly if the problem to be dealt with is one of world stagflation as one could if the policy being prescribed was for a country that was suffering an especially high rate of inflation by world standards.

Nevertheless, there is sufficient by way of *a priori* argument and empirical evidence (such as that in Tables 3.7, 3.8, 3.9 and 3.10) to suggest that *some* of the anti-inflationary effect of tight monetary policies (especially by comparison with tax increases) operates through domestic channels. It may therefore be argued that a mix with tight monetary policies (and appropriately lower tax rates) may be beneficial not only to the country applying the measures, but also to other countries and so the world economy – so long as high inflation is a concern of policy makers (rather than, or as well as, high unemployment) – provided that it does not have seriously adverse effects on thrift.

But there is another aspect of the use of tight monetary policy by individual industrialised countries or groups of countries that must be taken into account when considering macroeconomic policy from a global perspective. This is that one effect of tight monetary policy in major industrialised countries is presumably to hold down the prices of primary commodities (below what they would otherwise have been at the prevailing level of employment or the rate of real economic growth). This may be explained in various ways: but the channel of causation from monetary policy to prices described in Chapter 2 – whereby a rise in real post-tax returns on financial assets leads people to hold less by way of commodities that are in relatively inelastic supply, and to produce less by way of exhaustible resources at any given prices – may be at least in part the explanation for the effect of a tightening of monetary policy on primary product prices.

At any rate, whatever the manner in which this effect operates, high real interest rates tend to discourage the holding of stocks of commodities; and changes in the rate at which stocks of these commodities are accumulated or decumulated are important influences on their prices, relative to the prices of goods and services generally, and so on the export prices and terms of trade of primary-exporting countries.

As tight monetary policy tends to hold down commodity prices (at any given level of real output or employment), this is a channel through which price increases in the industrial world can be held down; but it obviously operates at the expense of primary producers – especially those in the rest of the world (producers, especially agricultural producers, *within* the industrialised countries often being protected by various types of support schemes, and as their interests are in any case likely to be given due weight by their own governments in deciding their macroeconomic policies). If so, part of the helpful effect of tight monetary policy in holding down inflation in the countries operating those policies is likely to be at the expense of smaller, less industrialised (and generally poorer), countries specialising in the export of primary products. So far as a reduction in the upward pressure on prices in the industrialised countries is brought about through this channel, it could therefore not be accounted as being helpful for solving the macroeconomic problems of the rest of the world, and would thus be less likely to contribute to the welfare of the world as a whole than to that of the industrialised countries adopting the mix. For its success in the industrialised countries would (to that extent) have been brought about through a channel that would tend to weaken the rest of the world, by depressing incomes and economic growth there, and causing depreciation of the currencies of the primary-exporting countries – which would tend to increase inflation in those countries (as well as probably tending to increase unemployment there, as they may consequently feel it necessary to hold down the level of expenditure there in the face of the fall in their export receipts).

The above argument relates to the choice of macroeconomic measures employed by the industrialised world to operate their economies at a given level of employment or real output. There is, however, a more general aspect of this same problem. If the industrialised countries endeavour to hold down inflation by reducing their own rate of economic growth below what they would otherwise have felt able to permit, this will tend to improve their terms of trade by depressing primary product prices (irrespective of the particular combination of macroeconomic measures employed to restrain the growth of real output). To this extent, the success that they may achieve in checking inflation by holding down real output will have been purchased at the price of increasing the macroeconomic problems of primary-exporting countries; and could thus not be accounted an improvement from the world point of view. It has been argued that most of the success achieved by European countries in checking inflation in one period in the 1970s came through this channel; though it has also been argued that domestic channels (through money wage rates) were also important. A reasonable view would be that both these channels are likely to play their part in reducing the upward pressure on prices when industrialised countries operate their economies at a lower level of activity and hope thereby to exert downward pressure on prices.[1]

But so far as the channel of operation is by way of reducing their demand for commodities that they import from other countries, this clearly acts as an especially depressing factor on the rate of economic growth outside the industrialised countries, and is unlikely to have a downward effect on inflation in those peripheral countries (at any given level of employment or real economic growth), as it tends to cause their currencies to depreciate. The use of policies that hold down growth in the industrialised world below capacity, with the aim of reducing inflation, can therefore be reasonably criticised from a global point of view. This makes it especially important from this broader point of view that the industrialised countries should choose combinations of macroeconomic instruments that minimise inflation *without* depressing real output and employment in their economies below the level that would otherwise have been feasible.

Moreover, policies that achieve the restraint of inflation without sacrificing real output and employment – not only in the industrialised world but also in the 'peripheral', largely primary-exporting, countries – are likely to be in the long-term interests not only of the world economy as a whole and of the peripheral countries but also in that of the industrialised countries. For a healthy rate of growth in the peripheral countries is of importance to the macroeconomic health of the industrialised world. (For example, the slow growth of the import capacity of Latin America in the last decade or two of generally weak primary product prices has been partly responsible for the difficulties that the US – the major supplier of goods to Latin America – has had in achieving a strong trade balance over that period.)

It may reasonably be asked why there should be a risk of the industrialised countries pursuing macroeconomic policies that would conflict with their own long-term interests by needlessly depressing growth in the peripheral countries through the adoption of deflationary policies in the industrialised world. But there are a number of reasons why the industrialised countries might adopt such policies, even though they might well in this sense be acting against their own long-term interests.

In the first place, policy makers are often concerned mainly with short-term macroeconomic effects – for example, holding down inflation immediately prior to the next election whereas it might be a long time before the industrialised countries feel the effects on their exports of achieving a reduction in inflation by a sacrifice of growth, when eventually the consequent downward effect on the export incomes of the peripheral countries leads to a reduction in those countries' demands for the products of the industrialised countries. If so, any adverse electoral consequences for the governments of the industrialised countries that result from the eventual fall in their exports to peripheral countries might be postponed for a considerable time.

In the second place, those indirect adverse effects on exports from the industrialised countries to peripheral countries ar not likely to be felt in the same proportions as each country's share in the deflationary policies that cause the weakening of the prices of primary products. Moreover, the countries that stand to gain most from the fall in primary product prices are not likely to be also those that stand to lose most from the reductions in exports to the primary-exporting countries.

Thirdly, even if the adverse consequences for exports from the industrialised to peripheral countries happened to be borne in the same proportions as the responsibility of each of them for the deflationary policies, a government adopting those policies could not know this in advance, and might therefore be expected to give less weight to the eventual loss of exports than to the more immediate benefit to it of the reduction in inflation. If the governments of industrialised countries consider such matters at all, they can (and probably will) always hope that the long-term adverse effects will be felt by some other country.

It is rather more likely, however, that a country such as the US or Japan, whose importance in world demand for primary products is large, will take account of the possibility of such indirect adverse consequences for them (through the effects of their policies on the ability of peripheral countries to import) than will the governments of most of the smaller industrialised economies – the combined effect of whose policies on the peripheral countries' ability to import may nevertheless be considerable.

The implication is that industrialised countries should agree, in the interests of all of them, not to try to hold down inflation by combinations of measures that operate largely by reducing the prices of primary products – the long-term adverse effects of which on exports to peripheral countries will be felt eventually by all of the industrialised countries.

The general conclusion should be that, in the global interest, as well as in their own medium-term to long-term interests, industrialised countries should not operate their economies below capacity with the aim of reducing inflation if that effect is to be achieved by way of downward pressure on world commodity prices. This is true irrespective of the combination of macroeconomic measures with which they implement the deflationary policies. They should thus seek to hold down inflation by appropriate mixes rather than by tolerating rises in unemployment and the consequent loss of potential output. But a mix that includes tight monetary policy is likely to have a greater downward effect on commodity prices (for a given reduction in real output or employment) than one that incorporates tight fiscal measures (which tend to *reduce* interest rates at any given level of employment, and to that extent make for a higher level of purchases of primary, and other, commodities for stocks at any given level of real output or employment than than does a mix that involves a tighter monetary policy).

In addition, a mix that includes relatively tight monetary policies will tend to reduce the flow of capital from the industrialised world to peripheral countries; and may therefore be expected to that extent to have further adverse effects on the peripheral countries, compared with mixes that do not rely so much on tight monetary policies. Moreover, the downward effect on capital outflow from industrialised countries that may be expected to result from a mix with tight monetary policy will not necessarily benefit the industrialised world, which may consequently fail to invest in projects in the rest of the world that would have been profitable if a mix had been adopted that did not raise interest rates so much in the industrialised countries.

Furthermore, anything that raises interest rates in the industrialised world intensifies the very serious problems of debt-servicing from which many of these countries are suffering.

In view of these repercussions on primary product prices, on their debt-servicing problems, and on the flow of capital to peripheral countries, a mix with tight monetary policy is especially open to criticism from a global point of views; and it may have adverse consequences in the medium to long term also from the viewpoint of the industrialised countries, once the repercussions on world trade and output, through the effects on peripheral countries, have had time to show themselves. Rather than relying on a mix with tight monetary policy, therefore, from the global point of view it would probably be preferable that the industrialised countries should place most weight on mixes that involve a choice of combinations of the various fiscal instruments that will hold up employment and real output while minimising the upward pressure on prices. Such mixes will, as we have seen in preceding chapters, also be less likely to have adverse effects on private investment than mixes that rely upon tight monetary policy.

THE MIX OF FISCAL MEASURES

Let us now consider the various fiscal measures that have been discussed in earlier chapters, from the viewpoint of their respective effects on the world outside the country adopting the particular combination of macroeconomic measures in question.

There is first the obverse of one of the arguments in the preceding section: if one compares fiscal measures in general with monetary measures, the argument from a global viewpoint would be that changes in fiscal measures that would reduce the upward pressure on prices at any given level of employment do not rely (as tighter monetary measures *do* rely predominantly) upon effects that operate through the effects of capital flows upon the exchange rate, and also on world commodity prices, to exert downward effects on prices at any given level or rate of increase in real output or employment.

The argument raised above – that one cannot from the global point of view make such a strong case for a mix including tight money (as a means of checking the upward pressure on prices at any given level of employment), as one can for an individual country – means that correspondingly greater reliance should (from this global point of view) be placed on a suitable mix of different fiscal measures for holding down prices without unnecessarily sacrificing output or employment.

In other words, from the global viewpoint there is a stronger argument than there is from the purely national viewpoint of individual countries to hold down the level of taxation, especially those taxes that tend to have a net upward effect on prices and on money wage rates, and at the same time to hold down the level of government outlays as a ratio of GDP, so long as governments are concerned to minimise the upward pressure on prices at any given level of employment or real output. The respective effects of these instruments on prices do not appear (on the evidence given in Chapter 3) to operate *mainly* through their differential effects on the exchange rate. There is therefore not the same presumption with these fiscal mixes as there is with a mix of relatively tight monetary policy (coupled with easier fiscal measures, especially tax cuts) that the benefit obtainable by an individual country from the use of an appropriate mix to hold down inflation will be offset, from a global point of view, by an additional upward pressure on prices as a result of the other countries' currencies depreciating.

This is borne out by the evidence in Chapter 3 relating to the relative effects of different fiscal measures on money wage rates; for this affords considerable support for the view that the relative effects of the different fiscal measures in holding down inflation operate to a large extent through this channel. Moroever, the tables in that chapter showing the relative effects of the different forms of fiscal stimulus on prices at a fixed exchange rate, also support the view that income tax cuts score more highly than increases in government outlays in minimising the upward pressure on prices for a given real stimulus, even apart from their relative effects on the exchange rate. For some countries, monetary policy still appeared on this evidence (relating to a situation with fixed exchange rates) to be more inflationary than tax cuts; and monetary policy did not appear on this evidence to be for any individual country generally superior to *both* these forms of fiscal instruments, even if the exchange rate were not free to vary.

The EEC simulations for different types of tax cuts imply that cuts in other types of tax would be even less likely than income tax cuts to exert upward pressure on prices comparable to that resulting from rises in government outlays; and though those simulations are not available on the hypothesis of a fixed exchange rate, there is no reason to believe that their superiority in terms of the combinations of prices and output effects results mainly, or even largely, from their relative effects on the exchange rate.

If it is true, therefore (as *a priori* arguments such as those in Chapter 2, and the empirical evidence of Chapter 3, suggest), that the effects of tax cuts and reductions in government expenditure (especially in government consumption) have their helpful downward effects on the price level (at any given level or rate of increase in real output or employment) mainly through *internal* channels in the country adopting them, rather than through the exchange rate, there is reason to believe that the world as a whole would benefit if all countries adopted such fiscal policies. Even if only one or a few countries adopted such a mix, there is good *a priori* reason (as well as the evidence of Tables 3.9 and 3.10) to believe that the downward pressure on prices through internal channels such as money wage rates resulting from such a mix is the main way in which it operates, rather than through the exchange rate – which might have had symmetrically offsetting adverse effects on other countries. Indeed, so far as a successful adoption of such fiscal mixes exerts downward effects on prices, and if that reduces the expected rate of inflation over the relevant period, that would probably tend to reduce nominal interest rates in the country applying the policies; and it is possible that this will lead to lower capital inflow to those countries, at any given level of employment, and thus perhaps even lead to nominal depreciation of those countries' currencies (if capital flows are responsive mainly, or even partly, to nominal, and not merely to real, interest rates). If so, there would be no offsetting unfavourable effects on other countries' macroeconomic situations to set against the benefits accruing to the country operating the policies; and if such policies enable the country in question to operate its economy nearer to full employment that it would otherwise have felt able to do, there is good reason to believe that non-inflationary world economic growth, including that of other countries, should then be promoted by its adoption of one of those types of fiscal mix.

THE MIX AND THE WORLD ECONOMY

If the ranking of the relative effects on private investment and prices for the world as a whole – or at least the industrialised part of it – can be approximately estimated from the simulations for the seven major OECD countries discussed in Chapters 3 and 6, Table 9.1 would give an indication of what the relative effects on these objectives would be for a one per cent stimulus to real GDP.

If the relative effects of these three instruments on these three objectives are approximately as indicated in Table 9.1 (the figures in which are the unweighted mean of the outcomes for the effects on private investment for the seven major OECD countries, derived from the simulations used in tables in Chapters 3 and 6), cuts in income tax and government outlays of an appropriate size will tend to raise private investment and output while exerting downward pressure on prices – even without any change in the setting of monetary policy. (If downward effects on total investment, private and public together, are to be avoided, the cuts in government outlays would have to be concentrated predominantly on government current expenditure outlays.)

Table 9.3 shows that there are also combinations of these three instruments that can raise output and private investment while reducing prices, either with a change of monetary policy in the expansionary direction or with monetary policy being tightened. For a group of industrialised countries that is large enough not to be concerned about its current account balance as such, but primarily with the objective of thrift defined to consist only of the level of investment, an easing of monetary policy has an especially strong comparative advantage in dealing with 'thrift' (on the present definition), and an appropriate income tax cut coupled with reductions in government outlays can be

Table 9.1 Effects on various objectives for 1 per cent stimulus to GDP for the average of seven major OECD countries (change in average level over five years)

	Output	*Prices*	*Private investment*
Cut in interest rates	+1	+2	+0.8
Bond-financed rise in government outlays	+1	+1	+0.1
Bond-financed income tax cut	+1	+0.7	+0.3

SOURCE: derived from Richardson, 1986 and 1987.

used to deal with the other two objectives. At the same time, if monetary policy is made more expansionary, there are also combinations of the two fiscal measures that can be used to exert downward pressure on prices, and an expansionary effect on real output, while leaving a net favourable effect on private investment; and from the viewpoint of the rest of the world, the combination of measures with the expansionary setting of monetary policy is less likely to have a depressing effect on their export prices (consisting as they do to a large extent of primary products whose world prices tend to be reduced by tight monetary measures to a greater extent than by a mix with easier monetary policy).

It is likely that the relative effect of the three instruments on the three objectives in the non-industrialised world is basically similar to that for the world as a whole, except so far as the latter operate through the exchange rate and the terms of trade of industrialised countries (by affecting commodity prices). But those qualifications imply that a tightening of monetary policy in the industrialised world would not be so likely to hold down prices in the peripheral countries as in the countries applying that policy; indeed, the consequent adverse effects on their exchange rates, as their export prices are reduced and as a reduction occurs in the net flow of capital to them, may well mean that there is more likely to be an upward effect on prices in those countries (as their currencies depreciate as a result of the weaker commodity prices, higher interest rate payments, and reductions in the inflow of capital to them). This means that, for the world as a whole, the mix with a relatively tight monetary policy is less likely to have a helpful effect in holding down prices than it is in the industrialised world. But, as Tables 9.2 and 9.3 show, on these (reasonable) assumptions the industrialised world can still move all three objectives in the desired direction without tightening monetary policy – and even while changing it in an expansionary direction.

Table 9.2 Policy prescription with two instruments

	Output	*Prices*	*Private investment*
Bond-financed cut in government outlays	−1.0	−1.0	−0.1
Bond-financed cut in income tax	+1.1	+0.8	+0.3
Net effect	+0.1	−0.2	+0.2

Table 9.3 Policy prescriptions with three instruments

	Output	*Prices*	*Private investment*
Cut in interest rate	+1.0	+2.0	+1.0
Cut in government outlays	−5.0	−5.0	−0.3
Income tax cut	4.1	2.9	+1.2
Net effect	0.1	−0.1	+1.9
or			
Rise in interest rate	−1.0	−2.0	−1.0
Bond-financed cut in government outlays	−1.0	−1.0	−0.1
Bond-financed income tax cut	+4.0	+2.8	+1.2
Net effect	+2.0	−0.2	+0.1

It may also be asked whether the relative effects of these three instruments on the three objectives *when the mix is occurring in the peripheral countries themselves* is likely to be very different from the effects of the same changes in policy if they are occurring within the industrialised world. We have no empirical evidence on which to base an argument that their relative effects will in this case be very different from those applicable within the industrialised world, except so far as the latter operated through affecting commodity prices. So far as that channel for holding down price increases is important for the industrialised world, however, one may reasonably argue that it is less likely to be significant for the peripheral countries, which are less likely to be able to hold down commodity prices by a tightening of monetary policy.

CONCLUSIONS

The argument of this book has been to the effect that there are various combinations of monetary policy, government outlays, and tax rates that can be used to work towards the achievement of three macroeconomic objectives – high growth (or low unemployment), a reduction in the upward pressure on prices, and 'thrift' – defined as the change in investment plus any improvement, or less any worsening, in the current account balance of the individual country operating the policy.

Similarly, for the world as a whole, provided that two or more of the various macroeconomic measures available have different effects on prices and on thrift for a given effect on real output or employment, there are combinations of measures that can work towards all of these objectives, though there are also combinations of them that are less likely to be helpful for peripheral countries, and so for the world as a whole, than to the industrialised countries applying those mixes.

The approach of the foregoing chapters is broader than that usually employed in the analysis of macroeconomic policy measures in that it provides for the possibility that each of the available measures may affect each of the macroeconomic objectives either in an upward direction, or in a downward direction, or that it may have a negligible effect on that objective; and that the ratios of the effects of each instrument on each objective (for a given effect on one of those objectives) need to be assessed and taken into account in policy formation, as those relative effects will often be important in determining the appropriate combination of changes in the setting of all the policy instruments. Different policy prescriptions will follow according to the combination of the ratios of these effects that applies in each particular country or group of countries over the relevant period, as well as according to the direction in which a government wishes to affect each objective, and the weight that it attaches to a given change in each of them.

This approach differs from that commonly adopted, which tends to assume, at least implicitly, that the effects of each available instrument on prices will be the same for a given effect on output or employment. This is the implicit assumption underlying any discussion or appraisal of policy that asserts or assumes that some sacrifice of real output or employment is needed in order to reduce the upward pressure on prices ('inflation'). But provided that there is even one macroeconomic instrument that is less inflationary than some other, for a given real stimulus, there is a combination of the two that can be used to give a non-inflationary, or price-reducing, stimulus. If there are some changes of policy that can provide a real stimulus while actually reducing the upward pressure on prices over the period of interest to the policy maker, it is clearly important to move those instruments in the direction that will facilitate the achievement of both objectives (a rise in output and a reduction in price increases), rather than in the direction that will take the economy further away from the achievement of those objectives.

If a government is concerned also with a third objective – that of the level of private investment, together with the state of the current account – it is clearly important to take account also of whether the combinations of measures most likely to promote non-inflationary growth will also be those most likely to promote this third objective. In general. both the *a priori* arguments and the empirical evidence of this book suggest that, *within* the mix of fiscal policy, the combinations of measures most likely to promote non-inflationary growth will also generally have upward effects on private investment (or on the level of private investment less any deterioration in the current account deficit); but that combinations of tight monetary policy with either reductions in government outlays or cuts in taxes – one of the mixes that may be expected to promote non-inflationary growth in the non-industrialised world – is more likely to have adverse effects on investment than other mixes (involving changes within the mix of fiscal measures) that may also be used to provide a non-inflationary stimulus. But even with the use of an expansionary monetary policy to promote investment, there are (on the available evidence) likely to be combinations of measures that can promote all three objectives; though there will also be other combinations of these measures that are likely to be able to promote the short-term macroeconomic objectives of the industrialised world (though less probably those of the world as a whole) that involve a *tightening* of monetary policy.

The main respect in which the arguments of this book differ from those commonly adopted is that they emphasise that, even if the level or rate of change in unemployment has effects on the rate of inflation or its rate of acceleration ('natural rate' or 'NAIRU' – Non-Accelerating Inflation Rate of Unemployment – theories of inflation) those are certainly by no means the sole factors that explain the upward effect on prices during a given period in any country. For the setting of macroeconomic instruments that accompanies that level of unemployment also has a bearing on the extent to which prices rise over the period of interest to the policy maker.

Furthermore, even if the prevailing level of unemployment is considered to be satisfactory, in the sense that the government is not attempting to reduce it, the principles discussed in this book can also be applied to minimising the upward effect on prices at that level of unemployment, or to increasing the level of investment (plus or minus the change in the current account of the balance of payments) at the same level of unemployment (or, of course, to both reducing the upward pressure on prices and increasing the level of investment or to improving the state of the current account at that level of unemployment). If the government is concerned with those aims, and not primarily with changing the level of unemployment or the level of operation of the economy relative to capacity, a combination of measures will generally be available that will hold down price increases and achieve an upward effect on thrift, while leaving the level of employment unchanged. Indeed, the likelihood of such a combination of measures being available is much greater when the government is trying to change only two of the macroeconomic objectives, while holding the third at more or less its prevailing level.

Moreover, some of the combinations of measures (changes in the fiscal mix) that are most likely to be able to provide a non-inflationary (or price-reducing) stimulus appear likely often to be also ones that will not tend to increase the fiscal deficit (or to reduce a fiscal surplus). In any event, it is not permissible to equate (as is so often done) the provision of a fiscal stimulus with an increase in the fiscal deficit: for there are some combinations of fiscal measures that will have the desired effects on those two macroeconomic objectives that will have a favourable effect, and others that will have an unfavourable effect, on the fiscal balance. Similarly, so long as different fiscal measures having the same effect on the fiscal balance have different effects on the current account balance, or on thrift, there is no presumption that reducing (or, for that matter, increasing) the fiscal deficit will tend to improve the current account, or to increase thrift. The so-called 'twin deficits' approach to the relationship between the fiscal balance and the state of a country's current account therefore turns out to be an unhelpful, and potentially dangerously misleading, guide to policy decisions.

In short, there can be no satisfactory approach to the choice of macroeconomic policy instruments that does not assess, and take into account, the relative effects of all the available macroeconomic instruments upon each of the various macroeconomic objectives that are of interest to the policy maker. An accurate assessment of each of those effects is not likely to be possible, but even an approximate estimate of their respective ranking in terms of the size and direction of their respective effects on each objective should suffice to ensure that the policy instruments are moved in directions that will contribute to the achievement of the objectives, rather than in directions that will make it harder to reach them.

Finally, in the interests of the world as a whole, as well as in their own long-term interests, it is important that governments should not only take into account the effects of the various combinations of policy on their own economy, but also take account of their likely repercussions on the rest of the world.

NOTE

1. See Beckerman and Jenkinson, 1986 and Grubb, 1986.

Bibliography

Beckerman, W. and Jenkinson, T. (1986), 'What Stopped Inflation – Unemployment or Commodity Prices?', *Economic Journal*, March.

Dramais, A. (1986), 'COMPACT – a Prototype Macroeconomic Model of the European Community in the World Economy' *European Economy*, March.

Grubb, David (1986), 'Topics in the OECD Phillips Curve', *Economic Journal*, March.

Fisher, P. G. *et al* (1988), 'Comparative Properties of Models of the UK Economy', National Institute *Economic Review*, No. 125, August.

Lindbeck, A. (1980), *Inflation: Global, International and National Aspects*, Leuven University Press, Leuven.

Perkins, J. O. N. (1979), *The Macroeconomic Mix to Stop Stagflation*, Macmillan, London.

Perkins, J. O. N. (1982), *Unemployment, Inflation and New Macroeconomic Policy*, Macmillan, London.

Perkins, J. O. N. (1985), *The Macroeconomic Mix in the Industrialised World*, Macmillan, London.

Perkins, J. O. N. and Tran Van Hoa (1987), 'Towards the Formulation and Testing of a More General Theory of Macroeconomic Policy', *Weltwirtschaftliches Archiv*, Band 123, Heft 2.

Richardson, Pete (1987), 'A Review of the Simulation Properties of the OECD's Interlink Model', Economic and Statistical Department, OECD, *Working Papers* No. 47.

Richardson, Pete (1988), 'The Structure and Simulation Properties of the OECD Interlink Model', OECD *Economic Papers*, No. 10, Spring.

Wallis, K. D. *et al* (1987), *Macroeconomic Models of the UK Economy*, Oxford University Press, Oxford.

Index